CW00361302

Contents

List of abbreviations

Courts

CJ: Court of Justice of the European Union (formerly the European Court of Justice or ECJ).

EWHC: High Court of England and Wales (also known as the High Court of Justice or High Court).

GC: General Court (formerly the Court of First Instance or CFI).

Offices

OHIM: Office for Harmonisation for the Internal Market.

UKIPO: UK Intellectual Property Office.

WIPO: World Intellectual Property Organization.

General

CTM: Community trade mark.
EU: European Union.
EEA: European Economic Area.
IR: International registration(s).
RCD: Registered Community design.

Statutes

Brussels Regulation: Council Regulation (EC) No 44/2001 of 22 December 2000 on jurisdiction and the recognition and enforcement of judgments in civil and commercial matters.

CAD: Directive 2006/114/EC of 12 December 2006 concerning misleading and comparative advertising.

CDR: Council Regulation (EC) No 6/2002 of 12 December 2001 on Community designs.

CTMR: Council Regulation (EC) No 207/2009 of 26 February 2009 on the Community trade mark.

TFEU: Treaty on the Functioning of the European Union.

TMD: Directive 2008/95/EC of 22 October 2008 to approximate the laws of the Member States relating to trade marks.

Foreword

This book of European trade mark decisions was first published in August 2011 and met with great success. Just over two years later, I am delighted to introduce the second edition.

European trade mark law continues to be a complex area, with new and important guidance being issued from the Court of Justice of the European Union on an almost daily basis. Aligning the laws of the various jurisdictions within the EU continues. This, combined with the possible introduction of the unitary patent and the Unified Patent Court, means that it has never been a more exciting or challenging time for IP owners on the long road towards full European harmonisation.

We have updated this book with decisions that have been overturned or upheld on appeal, and included new cases that are likely to have a direct impact on brand owners and their strategies for protecting and enhancing their trade mark and design portfolios.

Once again, I thank all of our contributors in both the D Young & Co trade mark and dispute resolution and legal teams for their dedication and hard work in putting together this second edition. We hope you enjoy reading it. Any comments, questions, criticisms or suggestions for our third edition, please don't hesitate to let us know.

Jeremy Pennant
December 2013

D YOUNG&CO
ABSOLUTE
GROUNDS

Chapter contents

DYSON

Dyson Ltd v Registrar of Trade Marks (UK)
C-321/03 , 25 January 2007

The mark, *per se*, did not constitute a sign and therefore it was not necessary to consider whether it was capable of graphic representation or distinguishing Dyson's goods from others.

Keywords
Absolute grounds; graphical representation; distinctive character; *de facto* monopoly; unfair advantage; Article 4 CTMR.

Issue
Dyson's application for two UK trade marks consisting of "a transparent bin or collection chamber forming part of the external surface of a vacuum cleaner" was refused and their appeal was rejected on the basis that the two trade marks were devoid of any distinctive character. Dyson argued that the marks were not devoid of distinctive character as they had a *de facto* monopoly in the goods which they had marketed for a decade and consumers would recognise that the goods came from them alone. The High Court referred the case to the CJ for a preliminary ruling.

Ruling
The CJ held that the subject matter of any application must be:

O a sign;
O capable of being represented graphically; and
O capable of distinguishing the goods/services of one undertaking from those of others.

The CJ found that Dyson had not applied for registration of the definitive 'bin' as the marks applied for were merely an example of such goods. As such, Dyson's monopoly of non-specific subject matter would obtain an unfair competitive advantage since it would prevent competitors from selling vacuum cleaners having any kind of transparent collecting bin on their external surface, irrespective of their colour or shape. Moreover, because of the non-specific subject matter, the mark was not a sign; it was merely a property of the product. Dyson's applications therefore failed at the first hurdle and could not be considered for trade mark protection.

BABY-DRY
Procter & Gamble Company v OHIM
C-383/99, 20 September 2001

This case established a low threshold for assessing distinctive character from which the CJ has now retreated.

Keywords
Absolute grounds; descriptive & non-distinctive marks; distinctive character; descriptiveness; Article 7(1)(b) & (c) CTMR.

Issue
Procter & Gamble (P&G) sought registration of the trade mark BABY-DRY in respect of disposable and textile nappies. The application was refused under Article 7(1)(b) & (c) CTMR on the basis that the mark consisted of a combination of two ordinary words with no additional elements that could be regarded as fanciful or imaginative, and immediately informed consumers that the products were suitable for performing their basic function of keeping babies dry. P&G appealed to the CJ.

Ruling
The CJ overturned the earlier decisions, pointing to the elliptical nature of the mark, its unusual structure and its "resistance to any intuitive grammatical analysis". The CJ found that BABY-DRY was an invented term which did not form part of the English language and was therefore unlikely to be used as a descriptive term.

Notably the decisions in DOUBLEMINT (page 11), BIOMILD (page 13) and POSTKANTOOR (page 170) suggest that the CJ will not follow this line of reasoning in the future.

COMPANYLINE

DKV Deutsche Krankenversicherung AG v OHIM
C-104/00, 19 September 2002

It is not sufficient to add together two words which are commonly used to achieve registration. Something more is required. Further, a trade mark must be wholly devoid of distinctive character to be objectionable.

Keywords

Absolute grounds; descriptive & non-distinctive marks; distinctive character; registrability; Article 7(1)(b) CTMR.

Issue

DKV applied to register the trade mark COMPANYLINE in connection with insurance and financial affairs at OHIM. OHIM refused registration on the grounds that it was devoid of distinctive character. The applicant appealed to the GC who upheld OHIM's decision and stated that the mark was "composed exclusively of the words 'company' and 'line', both of which are customary in English-speaking countries". The word 'company' suggested that the goods/services in question were intended for companies; although the word 'line' had various meanings, in the context of insurance and financial services it denoted a branch of insurance or line or group of products. Both were therefore generic words – coupling them together without any graphic or semantic modification did not attribute them with additional characteristics such as to render the mark distinctive as a whole. DKV appealed to the CJ

Ruling

The CJ, in turn, agreed with the comments made by the GC and upheld the refusal in its entirety.

DOUBLEMINT

Wm Wrigley Jr Company v OHIM
C-191/01, 23 October 2003

Under Article 7(1)(c) CTMR, a mark must be refused if at least one of its possible meanings designates, or may in future designate, a characteristic of the goods/services.

Keywords

Absolute grounds; descriptive & non-distinctive marks; descriptiveness; Article 7(1)(c) CTMR.

Issue

Wrigley applied for the word mark DOUBLEMINT for chewing gum. Objections were raised by OHIM under Article 7(1)(c) CTMR on the basis that the mark was descriptive of the nature of the goods.

An appeal was made to the GC on the grounds that DOUBLEMINT was not exclusively descriptive and was "ambiguous and suggestive".

The GC considered that for an English-speaker, the numerous meanings of the word DOUBLEMINT (for example, double the amount of mint or two kinds of mint) were immediately apparent but for a non-English speaker, the terms would have a vague and invented meaning. Therefore, as the average consumer would not immediately detect the description in relation to a characteristic of the goods, registration could not be refused.

Ruling

The CJ viewed the mark as being entirely factual and containing an objective reference to mint flavour in some way doubled. Also, the term would be perceived and understood almost immediately by the public and, as such, a flavour would be viewed as being a salient feature of the goods, chewing gum; thus, DOUBLEMINT did not qualify for registration.

If a mark is capable of being used by other economic operators to designate a characteristic of their goods and/or services, and is likely to be used as such in the future, this provides OHIM with valid grounds for objecting under Article 7(1)(c) CTMR. As a result, whether there is any unrelated third party use of the mark at the time of the application is not relevant.

STREAMSERVE

Streamserve Inc v OHIM
C-150/02, 05 February 2004

The link between the trade mark and the goods/services must be direct and specific in order for it to be objectionable as a descriptive mark.

Keywords

Absolute grounds; descriptive & non-distinctive marks; registrability; Article 7(1)(c) CTMR.

Issue

Streamserve filed for the trade mark STREAMSERVE in classes 9 and 16. OHIM refused registration on the grounds that STREAMSERVE, which is made up of two English words without any additional, unusual or innovative elements, was descriptive of the intended use of the goods concerned, in this case, a technique known as streaming.

The GC stated that the aim of keeping descriptive terms free from registration was in the public interest and such terms should not be reserved by one undertaking alone. The trade mark was considered from the relevant public's viewpoint as having a sufficiently direct link with the goods. The GC considered that the word STREAMSERVE was made up of a basic verb (serve) and a noun (stream) and was, therefore, not unusual for the consumers concerned. The GC refused Streamserve's appeal and the case was further appealed to the CJ.

Ruling

The CJ held that the descriptiveness clause, Article 7(1)(c) CTMR, was intended "not to prevent any monopolising of ordinary descriptive terms but rather to avoid the registration of descriptive brand names for which no protection could be available." In those circumstances, it considered the GC's test to be too severe in the application of those provisions to the facts of the case. However, this was not sufficient to overrule the decision and the CJ upheld the decision of the GC.

BIOMILD
Campina Melkunie BV v Benelux-Merkenbureau
C-265/00, 12 February 2004

A neologism must contain something more than two descriptive elements combined in order to achieve registration.

Keywords
Absolute grounds; descriptive & non-distinctive marks; neologisms; registrability.

Issue
Campina applied to register BIOMILD for various foodstuffs including milk products. The application was rejected by the Benelux Trade Mark Registry on the grounds that the sign BIOMILD conveyed solely that the products were biological and mild. The registry stated that the sign was thus "exclusively descriptive and does not have any distinctive character ... that finding is not altered by the fact that the two components are combined." The decision was referred to the CJ by the Benelux Court of Justice.

Ruling
The CJ held that a trade mark consisting of a neologism composed of elements, each of which is descriptive of the characteristics of the goods/services in respect of which registration is sought, is itself descriptive of the characteristics of those goods/services for the purpose of that provision unless there is a perceptual difference between the neologism and the mere sum of its parts.

To be registered as a trade mark the unusual nature of the combination in relation to the goods/services must create an impression which is sufficiently far removed from that produced by the mere combination of meanings lent by the elements of which it is composed, with the result that the word is more than the sum of its parts.

SAT.1

SAT.1 SatellitenFernsehen GmbH v OHIM
C-329/02, 16 September 2004

When considering the distinctiveness of a composite trade mark, for example a sign made up of letters and numbers, the correct approach is to adopt the stance of the relevant consumer of the goods/services for which registration of the mark is sought and then to consider the trade mark as a whole.

Keywords
Absolute grounds; descriptive & non-distinctive marks; devoid of any distinctive character; descriptiveness; Article 7(1)(b) & (c) CTMR.

Issue
SAT.1 sought registration of the trade mark SAT.2 in respect of satellite and satellite broadcasting services. Both OHIM and the GC refused registration on the basis of Article 7(1)(b) & (c) CTMR, finding that "SAT" was short for satellite, "2" was a number used in the presentation of such services and ".", being just a punctuation mark, had no distinctive character at all.

Ruling
The CJ disagreed, emphasising that there is no presumption that elements which are individually devoid of distinctive character cannot, on being combined, be perceived by the relevant consumer as being distinctive; there is no specific level of linguistic or artistic creativity or imaginativeness that must be shown before a trade mark can be registered. The only requirement is that the mark enables the relevant public to identify the origin of the goods/services and to distinguish them from those of other undertakings; the frequent use of trade marks consisting of a word and a number in the telecommunications sector showed that such a combination cannot be considered to be devoid of distinctive character, in principle.

It is inappropriate to divide up the sign into its component parts, find that each of those parts, by itself, is non-distinctive and then conclude that the whole mark cannot be more distinctive than the sum of its parts. The relevant assessment depends on an appraisal of the character of the trade mark as a whole.

NICHOLS

Nichols plc v Registrar of Trade Marks (UK)
C 404/02, 16 September 2004

The CJ appeared to favour a 'first come, first served' approach moving away from the restrictive approach to registrability of surnames favoured by the UK Registry. Objections should not be raised solely on the basis that a large number of people possess that surname. The distinctive character of surnames was more recently discussed in BARBARA BECKER (page 95).

Keywords
Absolute grounds; descriptive & non-distinctive marks; distinctive character; surnames; Article 7(1)(b) CTMR.

Issue
The UK Registry found that the surname 'Nichols', including its phonetic equivalent 'Nicholls' and its singular form 'Nichol', was common in the UK, given the number of times it appears in the London telephone directory. The mark was therefore refused in relation to vending machines and food and drink. The CJ was asked to review the UK practice in relation to common surnames.

Ruling
The CJ held that the assessment of whether or not a surname is a distinctive trade mark should follow the same criteria as are applicable to other categories of trade mark. Therefore, it is incorrect to apply stricter criteria than would otherwise be applicable. Pre-fixed guidelines for assessment, ie, the number of entries in a telephone directory, cannot determine this issue.

Notably, the perception of the relevant consumer must be taken into account. This may include considering the number of traders sharing that name within the relevant market, as this could affect the consumer's perception of the sign as a trade mark. Therefore it may prove more difficult to establish that a surname has a distinctive character in certain categories of goods/services than in others. However, surnames per se cannot automatically be regarded as unregistrable.

The CJ confirmed that traders legitimately operating under their own name can use this fact as a defence to a claim for infringement.

BIOID

BioID AG v OHIM
C-37/03, 15 December 2005

Two common elements joined together with commonly-used typefaces does not constitute distinctive character.

Keywords
Absolute grounds; descriptive & non-distinctive marks; registrability; overall impression; Article 7(1)(b) CTMR.

Issue
BioID AG filed an application to register the trade mark BioID.® for goods/services in classes 9, 38 and 42. OHIM rejected the application on the grounds that it was descriptive and devoid of distinctive character. The refusal was appealed to the GC who upheld the refusal and stated that the relevant public would understand BioID as meaning "biometrical identification" and from the point of view of the relevant public, the abbreviation BioID was likely to be commonly used, in trade. The graphical elements used, namely the typeface and the full stop and ® symbol were likely to be used in trade, to present all types of goods and services and were therefore also devoid of distinctive character.

Ruling
The CJ upheld the decision of the GC and confirmed that in order to ascertain whether a trade mark guarantees the origin of the relevant product or service to consumer/end user, it is appropriate to take the viewpoint of the relevant public. The CJ agreed with the GC assessment of the trade mark and concluded that the overall impression conveyed was that the abbreviation BioID was devoid of distinctive character.

MATRATZEN

Matratzen Concorde AG v Hukla Germany SA
C-421/04, 09 March 2006

A term which is borrowed from the language of another member state (where it is considered devoid of distinctive character) is not precluded from registration in another member state unless the relevant public in that other member state are capable of identifying the meaning of the term.

Keywords
Absolute grounds; descriptive & non-distinctive marks; registrability; foreign words; Article 7(1)(b) & (c) CTMR.

Issue
Spanish case law considers names borrowed from foreign languages to be arbitrary, capricious and fanciful. Therefore such names are registrable as trade marks, unless they resemble a Spanish word, making it reasonable to assume that the average consumer will be familiar with their meaning, or they have acquired a genuine meaning on the national market. As such, in Spain the word MATRATZEN can be a valid trade mark for mattresses even if it is the generic term for mattresses in Germany. The question referred to the CJ was whether that interpretation was compatible with the concept of the single market.

Ruling
The CJ held it is possible that, because of linguistic, cultural, social and economic differences between member states, a trade mark which is devoid of distinctive character or descriptive of the goods/services concerned in one member state is not necessarily so in another member state. The principle of free movement of goods does not affect the existence of rights recognised by the legislation of a member state in matters of intellectual property, but only restricts (depending on the circumstances) the exercise of those rights.

CELLTECH
OHIM v Celltech R&D Ltd
C-273/05, 19 April 2007

This decision is useful as it confirms the onus lies with OHIM to show a mark is descriptive if a valid objection is to be raised.

Keywords
Absolute grounds; descriptive & non-distinctive marks; distinctive character; descriptiveness; Article 7(1)(b) & (c) CTMR.

Issue
OHIM rejected an application for CELLTECH on the basis that the mark merely consisted of a grammatically correct combination of the two terms, 'CELL' and 'TECH' (an abbreviation of 'technical' or 'technology') and therefore would not serve as an indication of origin for goods and services relating to cell technology. As the Board of Appeal agreed, Celltech appealed to the GC who overturned the decision on the basis that:

○ the Board of Appeal had not established that the mark would immediately and unambiguously be perceived as designating activities in the field of cell technologies; and
○ the relevant public would see CELLTECH purely as an indication of the type of goods/services in question.

OHIM appealed to the CJ.

Ruling
The CJ held in Celltech's favour, endorsing the judgment of the GC that the Board of Appeal had not shown the mark applied for to be descriptive of the goods/services. The CJ also confirmed that the GC was correct in holding that the Board of Appeal had failed to establish that cell technology was a method of production of the goods or a supply of the services. The CJ confirmed that a trade mark which consists of a number of elements should not be rejected where each of its components may be found to be descriptive and must be appraised in its entirety when assessing its distinctive character. The CJ concluded CELLTECH was not descriptive.

Contrary to OHIM's contention that the prior analysis of each of the elements of a mark is an essential step, the Board of Appeal is required to assess the descriptiveness of the mark, considered as a whole.

EUROHYPO
Eurohypo AG v OHIM
C-304/06, 08 May 2008

The CJ reinforces established case law that two common elements joined together are not sufficient to render a trade mark distinctive.

Keywords
Absolute grounds; descriptive & non-distinctive marks; registrability; combination of two elements.

Issue
Eurohypo sought to register EUROHYPO in connection with various financial services in class 36. Registration was partially refused. OHIM held that the components EURO and HYPO contained a clearly understood indication of the characteristics of the services, and the combination of the two components in one word did not render the mark less descriptive. The decision was appealed to the GC who held that OHIM rightly found that the individual components 'EURO' and 'HYPO' were descriptive of the services. In examining whether the conjoined components also bestowed a descriptive character, the GC agreed and said, "… in the present case the word sign EUROHYPO is a straightforward combination of two descriptive elements, which does not create an impression sufficiently far removed from that produced by the mere combination of the elements of which it is composed to amount to more than the sum of its parts."

Ruling
The CJ upheld the refusal and also stated, "As regards a compound mark, such as that at issue in the present case, the assessment of its distinctive character cannot be limited to an evaluation of each word or component considered in isolation but must, on any view, be based on an overall perception of that mark by the relevant public and not on the presumption that elements individually devoid of distinctive character cannot, on being combined, have a distinctive character."

A

OHIM v BORCO-Marken-Import Matthiesen GmbH & Co KG
C-265/09, 09 September 2010

This decision could trigger numerous applications for single figurative letter trade marks and although each case is to be decided on its merits, the CJ appears to have set a precedent.

Keywords
Absolute grounds; descriptive & non-distinctive marks; single letter marks; Article 7(1)(b) CTMR.

Issue
The GC annulled the Board of Appeal's refusal of an application under Article 7(1)(b) CTMR. The sign in question was a figurative representation of the letter 'a' in respect of alcoholic beverages (except beers), wines, sparkling wines and beverages containing wine in class 33. OHIM appealed the decision.

The letter 'a' appeared in a fairly standard font (see above), although it was considered a figurative mark and not a word mark. The GC held that the Board of Appeal had erred in reaching the conclusion that single letters lacked the minimum level of distinctive character. The assessment that single letters should remain available to all was contrary to Article 4 TMD and the Board of Appeal had misapplied Article 7(1) (b) CTMR.

Ruling
The CJ said that it should be borne in mind that registration of a sign as a trade mark is not subject to a finding of a specific level of linguistic or artistic creativity or imaginativeness on the part of the proprietor of the trade mark. This was in line with the judgment in SAT.1 (page 14). The appeal was therefore dismissed.

STITCH DESIGN (POCKET)

Rosenruist – Gestão e serviços Lda v OHIM
T-388/09, 28 September 2010

This GC decision emphasises the difficulty in registering figurative marks consisting of decorative designs, particularly in relation to clothing and fashion goods. This case also highlights that the Board of Appeal may provide general reasoning in relation to all of the goods in question and that in this case at least, a differentiated assessment for each of the goods was not required, so long as the Board of Appeal provided an analysis of the perception of the relevant consumer of the goods.

Keywords

Absolute grounds; descriptive & non-distinctive marks; distinctive character; mere variation of a common feature; Article 7(1)(b) CTMR.

Issue

The mark applied for consisted of decorative stitching of curved lines applied to pockets; the unevenly broken lines representing the perimeter of the pocket to which the applicant made no claim and which only served to indicate the position of the mark on the pocket. OHIM and subsequently, on appeal, the Board of Appeal, held that the mark was devoid of any distinctive character under Article 7(1)(b) CTMR in relation to the goods applied for in classes 18 and 25. The stitching pattern was held to be a mere variation of a common feature of the goods concerned that would not enable the relevant consumer to identify its commercial origin.

Ruling

The GC upheld the Board of Appeal decision. The mark was devoid of any distinctive character in relation to the claimed goods. The GC agreed with the Board of Appeal's finding that a stitched pocket was a usual and commonplace feature of fashion goods and that the pattern did not depart significantly from the standard presentation of pocket designs. Consequently, the average consumer would perceive the stitching merely as a decorative feature and not as an indication of commercial origin of the goods. In this case, the mark did not possess the minimum degree of distinctive character necessary to achieve registration since it did not have any "memorable or eye-catching" features.

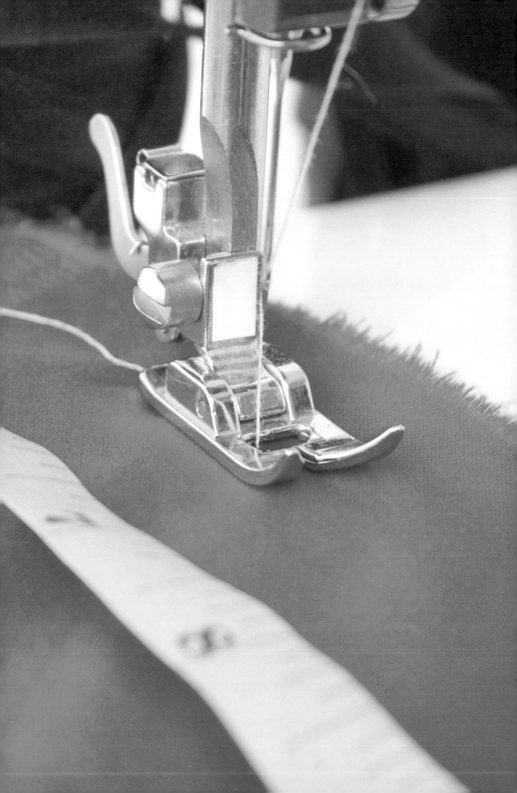

BETWIN

i-content Ltd Zweigniederlassung Deutschland v OHIM
T-258/09, 06 July 2011

This case provides a useful reminder to OHIM that a mark cannot be declared descriptive in the abstract. OHIM must provide adequate reasons for refusing a mark under Article 7(1)(b) & (c) against each item listed in the specifications.

Keywords
Absolute grounds; descriptive & non-distinctive marks; Article 7(1)(b) & (c) CTMR.

Issue
i-content applied to register the trade mark BETWIN for services in classes 35, 38 and 41, which included gambling, gaming and betting activities. OHIM refused the application as the mark was considered to be non-distinctive and descriptive. The Board of Appeal upheld the examiner's decision on the basis that English speakers within the EU would immediately perceive a direct link between the mark applied for and the services claimed. The applicant appealed to the GC.

Ruling
The GC ruled that the trade mark was descriptive for those services which provided the consumer with a direct link to gambling and/or betting. However, in relation to the remaining services, the mere fact that they fall in the same class is not sufficient to warrant their rejection on the same descriptive grounds. The GC considered that the services applied for fell into two categories; those which had as their main object the offer of gambling or betting and those which did not have any direct link with the gambling sector.

The Board of Appeal had failed to provide reasons as to why all of the services in classes 35, 38 and 41 were descriptive, and on that basis, the Board of Appeal's decision in relation to those services which lacked a full analysis must, therefore, be annulled. Furthermore, since the Board of Appeal had, essentially, said the mark lacked distinctive character because it was descriptive, meant the decision to refuse registration under Article 7(1)(b) CTMR must also be annulled in relation to those services which the GC considered lacked full analysis by the Board of Appeal as to their descriptiveness.

MULTI MARKETS FUND MMF

Alfred Strigl v Deutsches Patent-und Markenamt;
& Securvita Gesellschaft zur Entwicklung alternativer
Versicherungskonzepte mbH v Öko-Invest
Verlagsgesellschaft mbH
Joined cases C-90/11 & C-91/11, 15 March 2012

This case addresses marks consisting of descriptive
words combined with abbreviations for those words.

Keywords

Absolute grounds; descriptive & non-distinctive marks; descriptive words;
acronyms; Article 3(1)(b) & (c) TMD; Article 7(1)(b) & (c) CTMR.

Issue

The German Patent and Trade Mark Office (DPMA) considered the marks
MULTI MARKETS FUND MMF and NAI - DER NATUR-AKTIEN-INDEX
to be descriptive, consisting of three word elements that described an
investment fund and a share index respectively, combined with a three letter
acronym corresponding to the words. In each case, the German Federal
Patent Court referred a question to the CJ asking whether Article 3(1)(b)
& (c) TMD was applicable to a word sign which consisted of a descriptive
word combination and a non-descriptive letter sequence, where the letter
sequence is an abbreviation of the descriptive words so that the whole
mark can be seen as a "combination of mutually explanatory descriptive
indications or abbreviations"

Ruling

The CJ noted that the German court had found that the word combinations
were descriptive of the characteristics of the services but the letter
sequences/abbreviations, taken in isolation, were not descriptive. The
CJ commented that in each case, the combination of words and the letter
sequence had the purpose of clarifying each other and drawing attention to
the fact that they were linked. It was of no consequence whether the letter
sequence preceded or followed the words.

The answer to the question was that Article 3(1)(b) & (c) TMD is applicable
to a word mark which consists of the juxtaposition of a descriptive word
combination and a letter sequence which is non-descriptive itself, if the
relevant public recognises that the letter sequence is an abbreviation of
the word combination, and the mark as a whole can be understood as a
combination of descriptive indications or abbreviations which is therefore
devoid of distinctive character.

WINDSURFING CHIEMSEE

Windsurfing Chiemsee Produktions-und Vertriebs GmbH
v Boots-und Segelzubehör Walter Huber (C-108/97)
& Franz Attenberger (C-109/97)
Joined cases C-108/97 & C-109/97, 04 May 1999

This case established the so-called 'public interest' test
ie, descriptive words and signs should be freely available
to all and not subject to restrictions. It also raised the
issue of 'reasonable forseeability' for objections under
Article 7(1)(c) CTMR. It sets out useful guidelines for the
assessment of distinctiveness acquired through use and
the evidence required to support such a claim under
Article 7(3) CTMR.

Keywords
Absolute grounds; acquired distinctiveness; descriptiveness; geographical
indications; acquired distinctiveness; Article 7(1)(c) CTMR; Article 7(3) CTMR.

Issue
This case concerned the use of the designation 'Chiemsee' for the sale of
sportswear in the area surrounding the Chiemsee in Germany (the largest
lake in Bavaria).

Ruling
Article 7(1)(c) CTMR does not prohibit the registration of place names as
trade marks solely where the names designate places which are currently
associated with the category of goods/services in question, but also where
the geographical names are liable to be used in the future as indicators of
geographical origin of the relevant goods/services.

However, where the geographical designation has gained a new
significance as a result of the use made of it, it may be registered as a
trade mark. In assessing distinctive character, the following may be taken
into account:

O the market share held by the mark;
O how intensive, geographically widespread and longstanding use of the
   mark has been;
O the amount invested by the undertaking in promoting the mark;
O the proportion of the relevant class of persons who, because of the mark,
   identify goods as originating from a particular undertaking; and
O the statements from chambers of commerce and industry or other trade
   and professional associations.

PURE DIGITAL

Imagination Technologies Ltd v OHIM
C-542/07, 11 June 2009

For Article 7(3) CTMR to apply, a mark must have acquired distinctive character prior to the application date.

Keywords
Absolute grounds; acquired distinctiveness; use after date of application; Article 7(1)(b) & (c) CTMR; Article 7(3) CTMR.

Issue
The CJ was asked to set aside a judgment of the GC which had upheld a decision to refuse the trade mark PURE DIGITAL in classes 9 and 38 under Article 7(1)(b) & (c) CTMR on the basis that the mark was devoid of any distinctive character and was descriptive.

Imagination Technologies had filed evidence of acquired distinctiveness through use to support the application under Article 7(3) CTMR, but the evidence related to use after the date of the application and was therefore rejected. The applicant claimed that this evidence should be taken into consideration and appealed on this basis.

Ruling
The CJ held that the meaning of Article 7(3) CTMR was clear and should be interpreted literally as this is compatible with the logic of the system of absolute and relative grounds for refusal, according to which the date of filing of the application for registration determines the priority of one mark over another.

The CJ said that the GC was right to hold that the trade mark in question must have acquired distinctive character before the date of filing of the application.

Where objections of this nature are raised and use of the trade mark has just commenced, proprietors may need to consider re-filing at a later date and in the interim rely on their common law rights (where they exist) and use the 'TM' symbol until registration is secured.

THE PRINCIPLE OF COMFORT

OHIM v Erpo Möbelwerk GmbH
C-64/02, 21 October 2004

Whilst in principle a slogan should not be subject to any stricter examination in terms of assessing registrability, the success of the applicant in this case has not led to an obvious relaxation in OHIM's practice. OHIM continues to object to applications without taking precedents into consideration, usually arguing that the applicant has not shown that the public would be educated to view the slogan as a trade mark. Practitioners will appreciate that this is very difficult to prove for recently adopted or unused trade marks.

Keywords

Absolute grounds; slogans; taglines; registrability; distinctive character; Article 7(1)(b) CTMR.

Issue

The CJ was asked whether the slogan DAS PRINZIP DER BEQUEMLICHKEIT (meaning 'the principle of comfort') should be subject to the same tests and criteria as ordinary word marks when assessing its registrability. OHIM have consistently refused many slogan and tagline trade marks, regarding them as devoid of any distinctive character on the basis of their highly subjective assessment of the public's perception of the marks in question. OHIM appear to have notionally set three tests for slogan marks to overcome before they can be viewed as inherently distinctive:

○ They have the capacity to individualise/distinguish the goods/services of one undertaking.
○ They do not consist of signs or indications which directly describe the goods/services, or their essential characteristics.
○ No other reason exists which renders the slogan devoid of distinctive character.

Ruling

The CJ ruled that slogans may be seen as having an advertising function rather than indicating origin. The CJ said that the public is not used to relying on promotional messages to identify the origin of goods. However, an advertising slogan cannot be required to display 'imaginativeness' to have the minimal level of distinctiveness required under Article 7(1)(b) CTMR.

HAVE A BREAK

Société des produits Nestlé SA v Mars UK Ltd
C-353/03, 07 July 2005

The CJ's decision is a clear direction for National Offices of the EU to accept slogans or elements of composite marks on the basis of acquired distinctiveness through use on the condition that applicants can show that they are perceived as a trade mark by the relevant purchasing public.

Keywords

Absolute grounds; slogans; acquired distinctiveness; composite marks; Article 7(1)(b) CTMR; Article 7(3) CTMR.

Issue

Nestlé's application to register HAVE A BREAK in the UK was opposed by Mars who were successful on the grounds that it was devoid of any distinctive character. Nestlé appealed to the EWHC and then the Court of Appeal who took the preliminary view that the mark was only registrable if Nestlé could claim distinctiveness acquired through use.

The question referred to the CJ related to whether acquired distinctiveness could apply to use of a mark which is part of or used in conjunction with another mark.

Nestlé argued that merely because HAVE A BREAK was part of their better known phrase and registered trade mark, HAVE A BREAK... HAVE A KITKAT, this was no reason to preclude HAVE A BREAK from having acquired distinctiveness as a separate sign.

Ruling

The CJ confirmed that the acquisition of distinctive character through use must be as a result of use of the mark as a trade mark. It confirmed, however, that the mark in respect of which registration is sought "need not necessarily have been used independently". The CJ therefore confirmed that acquired distinctiveness may result from both the use as part of a registered trade mark (as a component thereof) and also use as a separate mark.

VORSPRUNG DURCH TECHNIK
Audi AG v OHIM
C-398/08, 21 January 2010

This is a useful precedent to use when the registration
of a slogan is sought and the examiner has reached the
conclusion that the mark is devoid of any distinctive
character, without providing valid grounds for objection.

Keywords
Absolute grounds; slogans; registrability; distinctive character; Article 7(1)(b)
CTMR.

Issue
In 2003 Audi's application to register the word mark VORSPRUNG DURCH
TECHNIK (meaning 'progress through technology') as a CTM was partially
refused on the basis that it lacked sufficient distinctive character.

The Board of Appeal dismissed Audi's appeal stating that the slogan conveyed
an objective message. The GC also dismissed Audi's subsequent appeal,
finding that the slogan was laudatory and that the relevant public would
perceive the mark merely as a promotional formula.

Ruling
Audi appealed further to the CJ, which found in their favour, some seven years
after the examination of the mark by OHIM. The CJ reiterated the fact that,
in line with previous case law, advertising slogans are not required to meet
stricter criteria than any other ordinary sign and 'imaginativeness' is not
necessary. The CJ held that the GC did not substantiate its findings to the
effect that the mark would not be perceived by the relevant public as an
indication of the commercial origin of the goods/services. The CJ commented
that a mark can in any case be perceived both as a promotional formula and
as an indication of the commercial origin.

Even if the slogan VORSPRUNG DURCH TECHNIK conveyed an objective
message, that fact would not support the conclusion that the mark applied
for is devoid of distinctive character. The CJ held that the slogan exhibited
a certain originality and resonance which made it easy to remember.

WIR MACHEN DAS BESONDERE EINFACH

Smart Technologies ULC v OHIM
C-311/11, 12 July 2012

This case reaffirms the principles in Audi v OHIM (VORSPRUNG DURCH TECHNIK page 30) but is an example going the other way – ie, a mark is devoid of distinctive character where it is not perceived as an indication of origin.

Keywords

Absolute grounds; slogans; registrability; distinctive character; Article 7(1)(b) CTMR.

Issue

Smart Technologies appealed the GC's decision to uphold the Board of Appeal's rejection of the word mark WIR MACHEN DAS BESONDERE EINFACH (meaning 'we make special (things) simple'). The mark was rejected as being devoid of distinctive character in relation to computer-related goods under Article 7(1)(b) CTMR. The appellant contended that the GC:

O Applied the wrong criteria when assessing distinctive character.
O Erred in law by categorising the mark as a slogan and considering distinctive character for slogans more difficult to establish than for other categories of marks.
O Erred in law by not concluding that a lower level of distinctiveness would suffice in this case, given the specialist relevant public.

Ruling

The CJ upheld the GC's decision. The GC had not misapplied the principles established *inter alia* in Audi v OHIM (page 30); to the extent that the public perceives the mark as an indication of origin of goods/services, the fact that the mark is at the same time understood - perhaps even primarily understood - as a promotional formula has no bearing on its distinctive character. The GC correctly concluded that the mark was devoid of distinctive character not on the ground that it was a promotional formula but because it was not perceived by the relevant public as an indication of commercial origin of the goods concerned. The GC, by describing the mark as a slogan, did not create a separate sub-category from other word marks or apply different examination criteria to assess the mark's distinctiveness. Further, the fact that the relevant public is a specialist one cannot have a decisive influence; a weaker distinctive character may not be sufficient where the relevant public is specialist. In the absence of evidence showing that the GC distorted the facts with regard to the assessment of distinctiveness, the third limb of the appeal is inadmissible and must be rejected.

PHILIPS v REMINGTON

Koninklijke Philips Electronics NV v Remington
Consumer Products Ltd
C-299/99, 18 June 2002

The CJ confirms the extent to which the relevant
legislation prohibits signs which consist exclusively of
the shape of goods necessary to obtain a technical result.

Keywords
Absolute grounds; shapes & 3D marks; necessary to achieve a technical
result; Article 3 TMD.

Issue
Philips objected to the use by Remington of a three headed shaver based on
their registered shape trade mark rights. Remington counter-claimed that the
shape marks were invalid.

Ruling
A shape cannot be registered as a trade mark if its essential features are
attributable only to a technical result. Moreover, such shapes cannot acquire
a distinctive character through use. Accordingly, although Philips had a *de
facto* monopoly in use and therefore consumers attributed use of a three
headed rotary shaver to Philips, this could not save the registration.

It does not matter if there are other shapes available which would achieve
the same technical result. If the shape is attributable to technical features
of the product, it cannot function as a trade mark. The CJ rejected the
argument that the availability of alternative shapes achieving the same
result takes the shape outside the prohibition.

LINDE/WINWARD/RADO

Linde AG (C-53/01) & Winward Industries Inc (C-54/01)
v Rado Uhren AG (C-55/01)
Joined cases C-53/01 to 55/01, 08 April 2003

Following this decision, registered Community design
protection is increasingly likely to be the most effective
route for applicants to protect new shapes and 3D designs.

Keywords
Absolute grounds; shapes & 3D marks; distinctive character; Article 3(1)(b)(c)
& (e) TMD.

Issue
These three cases concerned referrals to the CJ from the German Federal
Court of Justice. The applicants had in each case sought protection of 3D
shapes as trade marks depicting the goods themselves, namely a forklift
truck, a torch and Rado's application for a watch (respectively).

Ruling
The CJ confirmed that, as a matter of principle, the test for assessing the
distinctiveness of 3D marks should be no stricter than for any other type
of trade mark. However, Article 3(1)(e) TMD clearly indicates that there are
certain circumstances whereby shape marks will be refused protection,
namely:

○ Where they result from the nature of the goods themselves.
○ The shape of the goods is necessary to obtain a technical result.
○ The shape gives substantial value to the goods.

It should be borne in mind that the filing of evidence of use will not assist in
overcoming any of the objections raised under this Article.

The CJ also confirmed that in practice it may be more difficult for applicants
to establish distinctiveness in relation to a mark consisting of the shape of a
product than a word or figurative mark.

BAR OF SOAP
Procter & Gamble Company v OHIM
C-107/03, 23 September 2004

Where a shape is found only to vary slightly from other shapes used in the trade, it will not have the capacity to function as an indication of origin and will be considered devoid of distinctive character.

Keywords
Absolute grounds; shapes & 3D marks; Article 7(1)(b) CTMR.

Issue
Procter & Gamble applied for a 3D representation of a bar of soap with concave sides.

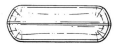

PERSPECTIVE
VIEW FROM ABOVE

PLAN VIEW

ELEVATIONAL VIEW
FROM ONE SIDE

OHIM rejected the application under Article 7(1)(b) CTMR on the basis that the mark was devoid of any distinctive character. Both the Board of Appeal and the GC agreed.

Ruling
The CJ found that the GC had correctly applied the criteria to assess distinctive character and would not interfere with the findings of fact made by the GC that the shape applied for did not differ sufficiently from commonly used shapes for soap.

MAG

Mag Instrument Inc v OHIM
C-136/02, 07 October 2004

The CJ held that only shapes departing significantly from the norm would be acceptable.

Keywords
Absolute grounds; shapes & 3D marks; registrability; Article 7(1)(b) CTMR.

Issue
Mag sought to register several 3D representations of different torches marketed by the company.

The Examination Division refused the applications on the basis of Article 7(1)(b) CTMR. The Board of Appeal and GC confirmed the Examination Division's decision and the matter went to the CJ.

Ruling
The CJ confirmed that average consumers are not in the habit of making assumptions about the origin of products on the basis of their shape or the shape of their packaging in the absence of any graphic or word element, and it could therefore prove more difficult to establish distinctiveness in relation to such a 3D mark than in relation to a word or figurative mark. Only shapes departing significantly from the norm would fulfil the requirement to indicate origin.

The CJ said that the fact that the torches in question were considered to be of high quality design did not automatically mean that they possessed the requisite level of distinctiveness. The CJ did make clear, however, that 3D marks were, if the requirements were met, perfectly capable of registration.

CORONA – BOTTLE OF BEER

Eurocermex SA v OHIM
C-286/04, 30 June 2005

The assessment of a shape mark is to be based upon the overall impression. The combination of non-distinctive elements is unlikely to be accepted for registration.

Keywords
Absolute grounds; shapes & 3D marks; registrability; Article 7(1)(b) CTMR.

Issue
Eurocermex applied for a 3D shape and colour mark for beers, mineral and aerated waters, fruit juices in class 32 and restaurants, bars and snack bars in class 42. The mark depicted a transparent bottle filled with a yellow liquid, having a long neck in which a slice of lime had been plugged.

OHIM refused the application under Article 7(1)(b) CTMR on the basis that the mark was devoid of any distinctive character. Appeals to the Board of Appeal and the GC were dismissed and Eurocermex subsequently appealed to the CJ.

Ruling
The CJ did not give a decision on the merits of the case, as the appeal from the GC was procedurally unfounded. The assessment of the mark was to be based on an overall impression of the shape and arrangement of colours. The decision of the GC was therefore upheld.

DEUTSCHE SISI-WERKE

Deutsche SiSi-Werke GmbH & Co Betriebs KG v OHIM
C-173/04, 12 January 2006

Registration of 3D marks is problematic since, by their inherent nature, they are likely to be considered devoid of distinctive character. Consumers are not in the habit of making assumptions about the origin of products on the basis of their shape or the shape of their packaging.

Keywords
Absolute grounds; shapes & 3D marks; distinctive character; Article 7(1)(b) CTMR.

Issue
OHIM refused registration of eight 3D marks consisting of different stand-up pouches for drinks on the ground that the marks were devoid of distinctive character.

The GC and Board of Appeal agreed and added that in the interests of competition there could be no monopoly in this type of packaging. Deutsche SiSi-Werke appealed to the CJ.

Ruling
The appeal was dismissed. The CJ found the GC was correct in assessing distinctiveness solely on the basis of the regulation rather than previous decisions of OHIM or the national offices, as both could be considered but neither had decisive weight.

A mark was considered to fulfil its essential function of indicating origin when it departs significantly from the norm or customs of the sector concerned.

WERTHER'S ORIGINAL (PART 1) SHAPE OF A SWEET

August Storck KG v OHIM
C-24/05, 22 June 2006

This case demonstrates the difficulties of securing acceptance of 3D marks, particularly where the mark is the shape of the product itself and is also packaged so that the consumer has limited (or even no) exposure to the trade mark at point of sale.

Keywords

Absolute grounds; shapes & 3D marks; acquired distinctiveness; Article 7(1) (b) CTMR; Article 7(3) CTMR.

Issue

August Storck (the makers of Werther's Original sweets) applied to register a 3D mark in the form of a light brown sweet for confectionery. The application was rejected for lacking distinctive character or acquired distinctiveness through use. Storck appealed up to the CJ on the basis that a stricter test for distinctiveness had been imposed for 3D marks than would have been applied to word or figurative marks, and that the lower courts had incorrectly applied the tests for demonstrating acquired distinctiveness through use under Article 7(3) CTMR.

Ruling

The CJ held that the relevant public's perception is not necessarily the same in the case of a 3D mark which consists of the appearance of the product itself, as it is in the case of a word or figurative mark which consists of a sign unrelated to the product it denotes. Although the criteria for assessing 3D marks is no different from other types of marks, the average consumer does not make assumptions about the origin of products based on their shapes. Therefore, it is in fact more difficult to establish distinctiveness for a 3D mark.

For the purposes of Article 7(3) CTMR, the CJ held that a 3D mark may acquire distinctiveness through use even if it is used in conjunction with another word or figurative mark. However, use of a 2D representation of the 3D mark (on the sweets' packaging) did not constitute use of the 3D trade mark and consumers did not actually see the shape of the goods when purchasing the sweets (which were of course wrapped and packaged) such that there was insufficient evidence to claim acquired distinctiveness.

WERTHER'S ORIGINAL (PART 2) SHAPE OF A SWEET

August Storck KG v OHIM
C-25/05, 22 June 2006

The CJ confirmed the difficulties of securing acceptance of shape marks on the basis of acquired distinctiveness since, if the objection is not language or country specific, evidence will be required for all member states of the EU.

Keywords

Absolute grounds; shapes & 3D marks; acquired distinctiveness; Article 7(1)(b) CTMR; Article 7(3) CTMR.

Issue

August Storck (the makers of Werther's Original sweets) applied to register a 2D representation of a sweet in a gold wrapper with twisted ends. The application was rejected for lacking distinctive character or acquired distinctiveness through  use. Storck appealed up to the CJ on the basis that an unduly strict test for distinctiveness had been imposed by requiring that the sweet wrapper be fundamentally different from other sweet wrappers commonly used in the trade, and on the basis that the lower courts had incorrectly applied the tests for demonstrating evidence of acquired distinctiveness under Article 7(3) CTMR.

Ruling

The CJ held that the lower courts rightly took into consideration the shapes and colours of sweet wrappers commonly used in the trade and could rely on their practical knowledge of such matters, without the need to provide concrete examples of third party uses.

For the purposes of Article 7(3) CTMR, the CJ held that the lower courts had also been right to require information regarding market share and advertising of the sweets, since the CJ thought it probable that the mark would only have acquired a distinctive character if the products bearing the mark had more than a negligible share of the confectionery market. Finally, the CJ confirmed that evidence of distinctiveness acquired through use should be provided for all member states, since a refusal would result if the mark was devoid of distinctive character in any single member state.

HENKEL'S APPLICATIONS – DISHWASHER TABLETS

Henkel KGaA v OHIM
C-144/06, 04 October 2007

The CJ once again confirmed that for figurative device marks which depict the actual goods applied for, acceptance will only arise when the shape departs significantly from the norm.

Keywords
Absolute grounds; shapes & 3D marks; figurative mark; distinctiveness; Article 7(1)(b) CTMR.

Issue
Henkel applied to register a figurative trade mark for dishwashing preparations and rinsing agents for laundry use.

OHIM refused registration on the grounds that it was devoid of distinctive character. Henkel appealed OHIM's decision up to the CJ.

Ruling
The CJ referred to the decision in WERTHER'S (pages 39 and 40) in which the criteria for assessing distinctiveness for 3D trade marks was discussed. The CJ said that account must be taken of the fact that the perception of the average consumer is not necessarily the same in relation to a 3D mark consisting of the appearance of the product itself as it is in relation to a word or figurative mark consisting of a sign which is independent of the appearance of the product it denotes.

Further, the CJ held that average consumers are not in the habit of making assumptions about the origin of products on the basis of their shape or the shape of their packaging in the absence of any graphic or word element, and only a trade mark which departs significantly from the norm or customs of the sector fulfils its essential function of indicating origin.

GOLDEN RABBIT SHAPE WITH RED RIBBON

Chocoladefabriken Lindt & Sprungli AG v OHIM
C-98/11, 24 May 2012

Lindt's 3D sign comprising a golden rabbit with red ribbon was devoid of distinctive character in relation to chocolate. Lindt failed to prove acquired distinctiveness in each member state where the sign lacked inherent distinctiveness. The existence of national trade mark registrations in some member states did not relieve Lindt of its obligation to show acquired distinctiveness in those states, as OHIM was entitled to make its own assessment.

Keywords
Absolute grounds; shapes & 3D marks; acquired distinctiveness; Article 7(1)(b) CTMR; Article 7(3) CTMR.

Issue
Lindt's long-running battle to register the golden bunny with red ribbon as a shape mark in respect of chocolate products resulted in an appeal to the CJ, in which Lindt sought to overturn earlier findings that the mark was devoid of distinctive character under Article 7(1)(b) CTMR and lacked sufficient acquired distinctiveness through use, pursuant to Article 7(3) CTMR.

Ruling
The CJ declined to interfere with the GC's conclusion that the mark did not depart significantly from the customs of the industry and accordingly could not fulfil the essential function of indicating origin. The existence of national registrations in 15 member states was not decisive and Lindt had failed to establish acquired distinctiveness through use in the part of the EU in which it did not *ab initio* have such distinctive character, namely throughout all of the EU.

SIECKMANN

Ralf Sieckmann v Deutsches Patent-und Markenamt
C-273/00, 12 December 2002

The 'Sieckmann criteria' have provided useful means
by which to identify the key elements of the graphic
representation requirement.

Keywords
Absolute grounds; smells, colours & sounds; smell (olfactory) marks;
Sieckmann criteria; Article 2 TMD.

Issue
Sieckmann applied to register a scent described as "balsamically fruity
with a slight hint of cinnamon" at the German Patent and Trade Mark Office.
In addition to this description, Sieckmann also provided a sample and the
chemical formula (pure methyl cinnamate, or $C_6H_5\text{-}CH = CHCOOCH_3$).
When the application was refused, the Office referred the case to the CJ.

Ruling
The CJ was of the opinion that signs which are not capable of being perceived
visually must be capable of graphical representation by utilising lines, images
or characters. The requirements were not met by a chemical formula,
a description written in words or deposit of an odour sample (or even the
combination of these).

The CJ set out what are now widely known to be the 'Sieckmann criteria',
which are that in order to be registrable, the representation of the mark must
be clear, precise, self-contained, easily accessible, intelligible, durable and
objective.

Although the CJ stated that the various methods used were not capable
of meeting the requirements, it did not make any suggestions as to what
methods were sufficient to meet them.

LIBERTEL
Libertel Groep BV v Benelux-Merkenbureau
C-104/01, 06 May 2003

Whilst the decision clarifies a number of points, namely that use of an internationally recognised colour code is almost certainly required to provide a clear and durable graphic representation, it is still not clear how marks which consist of a range of colours, or various shades of a colour, can be protected. The result is that further cases relating to colour marks are likely to be appealed to the GC and CJ for additional clarification.

Keywords
Absolute grounds; smells, colours & sounds; colour marks; graphical representation; distinctive character; Article 7(1)(b) CTMR; Article 7(3) CTMR.

Issue
Libertel sought to protect the colour orange by itself; shown on the form of application as a mere block of colour without any description in words or any reference to any colour code. Libertel's principal activity is the supply of mobile telecommunication services (it is now part of the Vodafone group).

Ruling
The CJ held that colours *per se* which are not spatially limited can be protected, provided that they are represented graphically and in a way that is "clear, precise, self-contained, easily accessible, intelligible, durable and objective", the 'Sieckmann criteria' (page 46). The CJ said that, other than in exceptional circumstances, it is unlikely that distinctiveness for colour marks can be demonstrated without prior use, especially where the relevant mark is limited to one colour. The CJ confirmed that the public interest is a factor which needs to be taken into consideration, especially where the applicant seeks protection for a broad range of goods/services.

SHIELD MARK

Shield Mark BV v Joost Kist h.o.d.n. Memex
C-283/01 , 27 November 2003

Shield Mark aimed to test the various options available to graphically represent sound marks. The ruling from the CJ gives clear guidance as to how to meet the so-called 'Sieckmann criteria' (page 46). A musical stave should be acceptable but a verbal description will not.

Keywords
Absolute grounds; smells, colours & sounds; sound marks; graphical representation; Article 2 TMD.

Issue
Shield Mark was the owner of a number of sound trade marks registered at the Benelux Trade Mark Office. One consisted of a musical stave with the first nine notes of the musical composition *Für Elise*, by Ludwig van Beethoven. Others contained a description and one consisted of the denomination "Kukelekuuuuu" (an onomatopoeia suggesting, in Dutch, a cockerel's crow) and the description "Sound mark, the trade mark consists of an onomatopoeia imitating a cockcrow".

Shield Mark sought to rely on their registrations in trade mark infringement proceedings in the Netherlands. This brought into question their validity based on the requirements for trade marks to be graphically represented according to Article 2 TMD.

Ruling
The CJ said, with regard to sound marks "those requirements are satisfied where the sign is represented by a stave divided into measures and showing, in particular, a clef, musical notes and rests whose form indicates the relative value and, where necessary, accidentals."

HEIDELBERGER BAUCHEMIE

Heidelberger Bauchemie GmbH
C-49/02, 24 June 2004

Colour trade marks are difficult to register and must be clearly defined. Descriptions cannot be vague and signs must be identified with certainty to achieve registration. Public interest considerations are also applicable.

Keywords

Absolute grounds; smells, colours & sounds; colour marks; graphic representations; colour combinations; Article 2 TMD.

Issue

Heidelberger Bauchemie applied for registration of the colour combination

blue and yellow as a trade mark in Germany. The representation of the mark comprised a piece of paper, the upper part of which was blue and the lower yellow. The mark was described as consisting of "the applicant's corporate colours which are used in every conceivable form, in particular on packaging and labels."

The application was rejected on the grounds that the sign was not capable of being represented graphically and was devoid of distinctive character. The matter was referred to the CJ.

Ruling

The CJ held that colours, or combinations of colours, may constitute a trade mark where, in the context in which they are used, those colours represent a sign, and the application includes a systematic arrangement associating the colours concerned in a pre-determined and uniform way. Further, even if a combination of colours satisfies the requirements for constituting a trade mark, it is necessary for the combination to fulfil other requirements of registration. Examination must also take account of the public interest in not unduly restricting the availability of colours for other traders.

FREIXENET BOTTLE SURFACE APPEARANCE

Freixenet SA v OHIM
Joined cases C-344/10 & C-345/10, 20 October 2011

Freixenet succeeded in this case based essentially on the GC not following case law to the letter. The CJ sent out a strong message to OHIM and the GC that they should go 'back to basics' when examining the registrability of unconventional marks and must provide reasoned justification for a refusal based on well-established case law on the subject. However, the CJ also confirmed that it remains difficult to overcome the test for establishing that an unconventional mark has the necessary level of distinctive character and "departs significantly from the norm or customs of the sector" so as to fulfil the essential function of a trade mark as an indicator of origin.

Keywords
Absolute grounds; smells, colours & sounds; surface appearance; distinctive character; Article 7(1)(b) CTMR.

Issue
Freixenet filed two CTM applications for the surface appearance of bottles of sparkling wine; one for a frosted white bottle and the other for a frosted black matt bottle. OHIM and the Board of Appeal rejected the applications on the basis that the marks were devoid of distinctive character in relation to the goods. On further appeal, the GC upheld the earlier decisions on the basis that the surface appearance (colour and matting of the glass bottles) could not function as a trade mark for sparkling wines.

Ruling
The CJ held that the GC had infringed Article 7(1)(b) CTMR by failing to consider whether the mark for which registration was sought varied significantly from the norm or customs of the sector. Although the GC correctly identified the criteria established by case law for assessment of marks consisting of the appearance of the packaging of the goods, the GC merely stated that since no bottle had been sold without a label, only the word element could determine the origin of the goods and the colour and frosting elements could not, by themselves and without the word element, function as a trade mark. Such an assessment would mean that marks consisting of the appearance of the packaging of the goods would be excluded automatically from protection conferred by the CTMR. The contested decisions were, therefore, annulled.

BRAVO

Merz & Krell GmbH & Co
C-517/99, 04 October 2001

Article 3(1)(d) TMD applies to all signs, but only where use of that sign has become customary in the relevant trade to designate the goods.

Keywords
Absolute grounds; customary (generic) marks; Article 3(1)(d) TMD.

Issue
Merz & Krell's application in Germany for the mark BRAVO in respect of writing implements was refused on the grounds that the word BRAVO is purely a term of praise. The relevant public would view the mark as no more than a laudatory term or advertising slogan, devoid of distinctive character.

Ruling
The CJ ruled that Article 3(1)(d) TMD must be interpreted as only precluding registration of a trade mark where the signs or indications of which the mark is exclusively composed have become customary in the current language or *bona fide* and established practices of the trade to designate the goods/services. Also, it is immaterial whether the signs or indications in question describe the properties or characteristics of those goods/services.

MAPLE LEAF

American Clothing Associates SA v OHIM
Joined cases C-202/08 & C-208/08, 16 July 2009

The presence of a national emblem, however small, is sufficient to warrant an objection to an application.

Keywords

Absolute grounds; national emblems; Article 7(1)(h) & (i) CTMR; Article 6ter Paris Convention.

Issue

The CJ was asked whether an application to register a representation of a maple leaf could be prevented on absolute grounds under Article 6ter of the Paris Convention concerning national emblems, which is given substance in Article 7(1)(h) CTMR.

American Clothing (AC) applied to register a mark consisting of the letters RW and a device of a maple leaf. This was refused by OHIM on the above grounds. AC appealed claiming that the maple leaf only formed part of the mark. The Board of Appeal dismissed the appeal and the case was further appealed to the GC. The GC decided that Article 7 CTMR does not apply to services, but nevertheless, the application had been filed in black and white which would allow AC to represent its sign in any range of colours, including a red-coloured maple leaf, and that there were no graphic differences from a heraldic point of view from the Canadian national emblem. Both AC and OHIM appealed to the CJ.

Ruling

In rejecting AC's appeal the CJ held that a trade mark which does not exactly reproduce a national emblem can nevertheless be covered by Article 6ter of the Paris Convention, as long as the mark would be perceived as an imitation of it. Moreover, Article 7 CTMR applies to both goods and services.

D YOUNG&CO
COUNTERFEIT
GOODS

PHILIPS & NOKIA

Koninklijke Philips Electronics NV v Lucheng Meihing Industrial
Company Ltd, Far East Sourcing Ltd, Röhling Hong Kong Ltd
& Röhling Belgium NV; & Nokia Corporation v HMRC.
Joined cases C-446/09 & C-495/09, 01 December 2011

Good imported from outside of the EU, which are imitations
of goods protected by rights in the EU, cannot be classified
as counterfeit or pirated merely because they have been
detained by customs in the EU in absence of evidence that
the goods are directed towards EU consumers.

Keywords
Counterfeit goods; customs procedures; detention of goods in the EU.

Issue
PHILIPS: Customs in Belgium seized a consignment of suspected
counterfeit shavers from China. Philips initiated an infringement action
against the manufacturer, shipper and forwarding agent. The only
defendant, the shipper, argued that the goods could not be detained and
classified as infringing goods in absence of any evidence that the goods
would be put on sale in the EU.

NOKIA: HM Revenue & Customs (HMRC) seized a consignment of
suspected infringing mobile phones from Hong Kong destined for Colombia.
Nokia confirmed they were counterfeit and requested HMRC to detain
them. HMRC refused because the goods were destined for a non-EU
country and there was no evidence to suggest that the goods would be put
on the market in the EU.

Ruling
Customs must detain goods where there is:

○ a lack of information regarding the identity of the manufacturer, consignor
  or consignee;
○ a lack of knowledge regarding the goods' destination;
○ a lack of cooperation with the customs authorities; or
○ a discovery of documents or information that the goods in question are
  liable to be diverted to consumers in the EU.

Precautionary measures may be utilised to facilitate immediate seizure of
goods posing a risk to health or safety regardless of whether they are directed
towards EU consumers.

D YOUNG&CO
DOMAIN NAME
DISPUTES

FIVEALIVE.CO.UK

The Coca-Cola Company v Bo Cat/Mr Paolo Ciuffa
D00008348, 06 June 2010

A domain name that is identical to a very well-known trade mark may not be considered an abusive registration if the respondent has a proper motive for the registration, supported by evidence. The burden of proof, therefore, rests squarely on the complainant to prove there is morally reprehensible behaviour on the part of the respondent.

Keywords
Domain name disputes; abusive registration.

Issue
Coca-Cola brought an action against Mr Ciuffa who had registered the disputed domain name in his company's name, Bo Cat. Coca-Cola has used the trade mark FIVE ALIVE in the UK since the 1980s. Through their use, they have acquired goodwill and a reputation. Coca-Cola argued that Mr Ciuffa had no legitimate interest in the domain name and given the well-known FIVE ALIVE trade mark, the registration of the domain name was made by Mr Ciuffa to purely capitalise on Coca-Cola's goodwill and disrupt its legitimate business interests. This amounted to an abusive registration. In his response, Mr Ciuffa claimed that he had registered the Domain Name with the sole intention of representing and promoting the music artist MC Five Alive. He provided evidence in the form of a MySpace link and recent flyers of MC Five Alive's performances. He denied that the Domain Name was an abusive registration.

Ruling
The expert said that there was little doubt that Coca-Cola had rights in the trade mark FIVE ALIVE. However, an abusive registration is one that takes unfair advantage of, or is unfairly detrimental to Coca-Cola's rights and a domain name can only be considered abusive if there is something morally reprehensible in Mr Ciuffa's behaviour. In this case, it was held that there was a perfectly plausible and legitimate explanation for the registration, supported with evidence, and the expert was given no reason to disbelieve Mr Ciuffa.

SMARTYHADAPARTY.CO.UK
Smarty Had a Party LLC v T AS Akinropo Ltd
D00010201 , 06 January 2012

This case highlights the need for a respondent to fully explain its motives and provide evidence to refute that its domain name amounts to an abusive registration.

Keywords
Domain name disputes; abusive registration.

Issue
T AS Akinropo Ltd (Akinropo) registered the identical domain name to US and CTM registrations owned by Smarty Had a Party LLC (Smarty) for SMARTY HAD A PARTY. During proceedings, Smarty showed that their website had been copied and Akinropo had even made multiple orders from their website. They also made reference to a number of emails and orders handled by their customer service department showing a number of customers had been confused by Akinropo's website. Akinropo was unable to fully explain why it had adopted the domain name; they claimed they had conducted due diligence such as searching UK copyright registrations prior to adopting the domain name, but no evidence of any searching was presented.

Ruling
The expert found that Smarty had established its earlier rights but whilst their evidence of actual confusion was unconvincing, there was enough evidence to point to a likelihood of confusion. Akinropo's reluctance to explain why it had chosen the doman name, a lack of evidence to support the due diligence it had carried out together with evidence that it knew of Smarty's business in the US pointed to foul play. For these reasons, the domain name was held an abusive registration and the transfer to Smarty was ordered.

WORKBOX.CO.UK

Box Clever Projects Ltd v Mr Garth Piesse
D00010593 , 07 February 2012

If there is no obvious use of an earlier trade mark registration which is identical to the disputed domain name and the domain name owner was unaware of its existence, there is no abusive registration.

Keywords

Domain name disputes; abusive registration; knowledge and awareness of earlier rights.

Issue

Box Clever Projects Ltd (Box Clever), is the owner of a UK trade mark registration for WORK BO X and three domain names for WORKBOX. Box Clever made several attempts to purchase the disputed domain name from Mr Piesse, all of which were rejected by him. Box Clever filed a complaint at Nominet on the basis of its earlier UK registration and domain names. It alleged that the domain name was an abusive registration because Mr Piesse is a serial purchaser of domain names and he had no justified reason to purchase the domain name other than for re-sale to Box Clever for profit.

Ruling

The expert found in favour of Mr Piesse. Whilst Box Clever had earlier rights, the registration of the domain name did not amount to an abusive registration. The expert accepted Mr Piesse's assertions that he had no knowledge of Box Clever or their earlier rights; there was no obvious use of the trade name WORKBOX or WORK BO X on any website and Mr Piesse was highly unlikely to have come across the use presented in Box Clever's evidence.

The expert also stated that Mr Piesse was entitled to buy and register domain names for re-sale and this activity in itself would not amount to abusive behaviour. Further, the domain name is a generic or descriptive term so in the absence of evidence to the contrary, it cannot be said that Mr Piesse bought the domain name to specifically target the Box Clever for the purposes of re-sale.

D YOUNG&CO
GEOGRAPHICAL
INDICATIONS

COGNAC
Bureau national interprofessionnel du Cognac (BNIC)
v Gust. Ranin Oy
Joined cases C-4/10 & C-27/10, 14 July 2011

In the case of a national trade mark registration which
contains a geographical indication (GI) (Cognac) with
respect to goods which do not meet the specifications set
out for that GI, the competent national authorities must
refuse or invalidate the registration of such a mark.

Keywords
Geographical indications; GIs relating to spirit drinks; invalidity; Article 3(1)(g)
TMD; Article 3(2)(a) TMD; Article 16 Regulation 110/2008; Article 23(1)
Regulation 110/2008; Article 23(2) Regulation 110/2008.

Issue
Gust, a Finnish company, applied in 2001 for two figurative marks in the form of a
bottle label incorporating the word COGNAC in class 33. Following opposition by
BNIC, the two marks were eventually registered but following appeals up to the
Finnish Supreme Administrative Court, a number of questions were referred to
the CJ for a preliminary ruling. The principal basis of BNIC's objection was that
the registration or use of the trade marks in connection with spirit drinks, which
did not comply with the GI specification, infringed Article 16 of Regulation
110/2008 (the 'Spirits Regulation') and such registrations were therefore liable to
be refused or invalidated pursuant to Article 23(1) Regulation 110/2008. The
Finnish court sought the CJ's ruling on *inter alia*:

O whether the Spirits Regulation is applicable to the assessment of the validity
   of a trade mark registration containing a GI protected by that regulation, where
   registration took place before the Spirits Regulation entered into force; and
O whether Articles 16 and 23 of the Spirits Regulation preclude registration
   where the mark contains a protected GI and is registered for spirit drinks
   which do not satisfy the conditions for use of that GI.

Ruling
The CJ ruled that the Spirits Regulation **is** applicable to the assessment of
the validity of a trade mark which **was** registered before the regulation
entered into force. Secondly, the Finnish authorities must refuse or invalidate
a trade mark registration where use of that mark would lead to one of the
situations in Article 16 Regulation 110/2008. Further, a mark registered in
respect of spirit drinks which do not meet the relevant GI specifications falls
within Article 16 Regulation 110/2008.

D YOUNG&CO
INFRINGEMENT&
OPPOSITION
GROUNDS

Chapter contents

ARSENAL v REED

Arsenal Football Club Plc v Matthew Reed
C-206/01, 12 November 2002

Infringement may still arise even when goods are marked as 'unofficial'.

Keywords
Infringement & opposition grounds; double identity; trade mark use; post-sale confusion; Article 5(1)(a) TMD; Article 6 TMD.

Issue
Mr Reed sold unofficial Arsenal merchandise. The case turned on the issue of whether a trade mark owner must establish that an unauthorised vendor is using the registered trade mark 'in a trade mark sense' to succeed in an infringement action. In the original UK proceedings Mr Justice Laddie found, as a matter of fact, that Reed's use of the Arsenal trade marks would be perceived by consumers as a badge of support or allegiance rather than an indication of the origin of the goods. The case was referred to the CJ.

Ruling
The CJ said that for infringement to arise trade mark use is required and made a finding of fact to the effect that Reed's use of the marks created the impression that there was a material link in the course of trade between the goods concerned and the trade mark proprietor. Accordingly, the CJ held that Mr Reed had infringed Arsenal's trade marks.

When the case returned to the UK High Court, Mr Justice Laddie held that in making a contrary finding of fact, the CJ had exceeded its jurisdiction. Applying the CJ's guidance on the law, but disregarding conclusions reached on the facts, he then dismissed Arsenal's claim for trade mark infringement. (On further appeal the Court of Appeal reversed the High Court's decision agreeing with the CJ, and finding that infringement had occured. See [2003] RPC 39, [2003] 3All ER 865).

THE GUNNERS

Arsenal

Victoria Concordia Crescit

ARTHUR ET FÉLICIE

LTJ Diffusion SA v Sadas Vertbaudet SA
C-291/00, 20 March 2003

Whilst the CJ applied a strict identity concept, complete identity may not be necessary when taking into account imperfect recollection. Two marks might therefore be deemed identical where there are differences so insignificant that they may go unnoticed by the average consumer.

Keywords

Infringement & opposition grounds; double identity; identical marks/signs; Article 5(1)(a) TMD.

Issue

LTJ Diffusion were owners of the trade mark ARTHUR in hand written form by way of a French registration and an international registration designating Germany, Austria, Spain and Benelux.

Sadas applied to register the trade mark ARTHUR ET FÉLICIE in respect of similar goods. The opposition that followed was successful before OHIM whose decision was upheld by the Third Board of Appeal. Sadas subsequently appealed to the GC and up to the CJ.

Ruling

The CJ held that, upon a comparison of the marks, identity had to be interpreted strictly. Insignificant differences between the signs may go unnoticed by the average consumer but, on the whole, a sign is identical with the trade mark where it reproduces, without any modification or addition, all the elements constituting the trade mark.

CÉLINE

Céline SARL v Céline SA
C-17/06, 11 September 2007

Use of a registered trade mark as a company/shop name
is not likely to be deemed use 'in relation to' the goods
unless it is also fixed to them.

Keywords
Infringement & opposition grounds; double identity; use; use of company/
shop name; Article 5(1)(a) TMD.

Issue
Céline SA owned registrations of the mark CÉLINE in connection with clothes
and shoes. When Céline SA commenced trade mark infringement proceedings
against Céline SARL, which had registered its company name and used it to
market ready-to-wear garments and various accessories, the question was
referred to the CJ.

Ruling
The purpose of a company name is to identify a company, whereas the purpose
of a trade/shop name is to designate a business that is being carried on. Where
use of a company/trade or shop name is limited to identifying a company or
designating a business, such use cannot be considered as being 'in relation
to goods/services' within the meaning of Article 5(1) TMD.

Four conditions were established by the CJ in relation to infringement of an
identical trade mark under Article 5(1)(a) TMD. Use must be:

○ In the course of trade.
○ Without the consent of the trade mark owner.
○ In respect of identical goods/services.
○ In such a way as to be liable to affect the functions of the trade mark,
    in particular its essential function to guarantee the origin of the goods/
    services.

L'OREAL v EBAY

L'Oréal SA & Others v eBay & Others
C-324/09, 12 July 2011

Operators of online market places may rely on Article 14 of
the E-Commerce Directive where they have not played an
active role in the data stored on its website, had no
awareness that the items for sale were unlawful and/or
acted expeditiously in removing the content.

Keywords

Infringement & opposition grounds; e-commerce; liability of online
marketplace operators; Article 14 Directive 2000/31/EC ('E-Commerce
Directive'); Article 11 Directive 2004/48/EC ('Enforcement Directive').

Issue

L'Oréal brought trade mark infringement proceedings regarding sales of
counterfeit and/or infringing products on eBay. Numerous questions were
referred to the CJ, including whether:

O the operator of an online marketplace escapes liability under Article 14 of
   the E-Commerce Directive as an Internet Service Provider hosting
   information at the request of the recipient of its services; and
O injunctions are available against intermediaries, such as eBay, whose
   services are used by third parties to infringe IP rights.

Ruling

The operator of an online marketplace may rely on Article 14 of the E-Commerce
Directive where it "has not played an active role allowing it to have knowledge or
control of the data stored" which involves providing "assistance which entails, in
particular, optimising the presentation of the offers for sale in question or
promoting them". The defence will not apply where the operator was aware of
facts or circumstances on the basis of which a diligent economic operator should
have realised that the offers for sale were unlawful or where it became aware but
failed to act expeditiously to remove or disable access.

While online intermediaries could not be ordered to actively monitor the data of
each customer for infringement, they may be ordered to take measures to make it
easier to identify sellers. Under Article 11 of the Enforcement Directive, operators
of an online marketplace may be ordered to take measures to bring both past and
future infringements of IP rights to an end. Such injunctions must be "effective,

WINTERSTEIGER

Wintersteiger AG v Products 4U Sondermaschinenbau Gmbh
C-523/10, 19 April 2012

In the context of keyword advertising, Article 5(3) Brussels Regulation can be interpreted so that, where an identical sign is used in a member state other than where it is registered, an action can be brought either in the place of establishment of the advertiser or in the member state where the mark is registered.

Keywords
Infringement & opposition grounds; jurisdiction; Article 5(3) Brussels Regulation.

Issue
Wintersteiger owned an Austrian trade mark registration for WINTERSTEIGER. Its German competitor, Products 4U, reserved the AdWord WINTERSTEIGER for use on Google's German top-level domain (google.de) but not on the Austrian equivalent (google.at). Wintersteiger commenced infringement proceedings and sought an injunction in Austria claiming that Products 4U's use of the keyword on google.de infringed its Austrian mark because google.de can also be accessed from Austria and the referencing service is configured in German. It argued that the Austrian courts had jurisdiction on the basis of Article 5(3) Brussels Regulation, which provides that a person domiciled in a member state may, in matters relating to tort, be sued before the courts of another member state 'where the harmful event occurred or may occur'. This is an exception to the key principle of the rules of EU jurisdiction that a person domiciled in a member state shall be sued in its country of domicile. The matter was referred to the CJ for a preliminary ruling.

Ruling
The CJ confirmed that the last phrase of Article 5(3) Brussels Regulation means both:

○ the place where the damage occurred (ie, where a national mark is relied on, the member state in which it is registered); and

○ the place where the event giving rise to the damage occurred (in this case, where "the activation by the advertiser of the technical process displaying… the advertisement" takes place, ie, the place of establishment of Products 4U).

SABEL v PUMA

Sabel BV v Puma AG, Rudolf Dassler Sport
C-251/95, 11 November 1997

This case established the fundamental standard for
assessing likelihood of confusion, setting out the global
appreciation test, the influence of the average consumer
and the impact of distinctive character.

Keywords
Infringement & opposition grounds; likelihood of confusion; likelihood of
association; average consumer; Article 4(1)(b) TMD; Article 5(1) TMD; Article
8(1)(b) CTMR; Article 9(1)(b) CTMR.

Issue
Puma objected to Sabel's application in Germany for a "bounding feline"
together with the word "Sabel", relying on their earlier trade marks depicting
a bounding feline (with no text) for identical/similar goods. The German court
referred the case to the CJ.

Ruling
The CJ held that: "The likelihood of confusion must...be appreciated globally,
taking into account all factors relevant to the circumstances of the case...
based on the overall impression given by the marks, bearing in mind,
in particular, their distinctive and dominant components".

Mere association alone was not enough to justify a finding of a likelihood of
confusion. The concept of likelihood of association was not an alternative to
a finding of likelihood of confusion. A likelihood of confusion has to take into
account visual, aural, and conceptual similarity. The more distinctive the
earlier mark, (either *per se* or because of the reputation it enjoys) the greater
the likelihood of confusion.

The perception of the marks in the mind of the average consumer of the
goods/services in question plays a decisive role in the global appreciation
test. The average consumer normally perceives a mark as a whole and does
not analyse its various details.

CANON

Canon Kabushiki Kaisha v Metro-Goldwyn-Mayer Inc
C-39/97, 29 September 1998

Indirect or economic confusion (where the public assumes that the relevant goods/services come from linked undertakings) is a valid form of confusion, even where there is no direct confusion between the products.

Keywords
Infringement & opposition grounds; likelihood of confusion; reputation; economic confusion; Article 4(1)(b) TMD.

Issue
The German court had dismissed an opposition brought by Canon against an application by MGM for registration of the mark CANNON. The argument focused on whether the goods for which MGM sought registration were sufficiently similar to the goods for which Canon had registered its mark CANON. The CANON mark was recognised as having a significant reputation.

Ruling
The CJ held that the distinctive character of the earlier trade mark, and in particular its reputation, must be taken into account when determining whether the similarity of the goods/services is sufficient to give rise to a likelihood of confusion.

When assessing the similarity of the goods/services concerned all relevant factors should be taken into account. Those factors include, *inter alia*, their nature, their end users and their method of use and whether they are in competition with each other or are complimentary.

A global assessment of the likelihood of confusion implies some interdependence between the relevant factors. A lesser degree of similarity between the goods/services may be offset by a greater degree of similarity between the marks, and *vice versa*.

Also there can be no likelihood of confusion where it does not appear that the public could believe that the goods/services come from the same or economically-linked undertakings.

LLOYD SCHUHFABRIK

Lloyd Schuhfabrik Meyer & Co Gmbh v Klijsen Handel BV
C-342/97, 22 June 1999

This case is commonly referred to alongside SABEL v
PUMA (page 78) and CANON (page 80) when assessing
the likelihood of confusion. A global assessment of the
mark and all facts relating to the case should be made,
taking into account the average consumer of the goods/
services in question.

Keywords
Infringement & opposition grounds; likelihood of confusion; aural similarity;
Article 5(1)(b) TMD.

Issue
Lloyd manufactured shoes under the trade mark LLOYD. Klijsen also
manufactured shoes and marketed shoes under the trade mark LOINT'S
and sought to register the mark LOINT'S. Lloyd sought to restrain Klijsen
from using the trade mark in Germany claiming that LOINT'S was likely to
be confused with LLOYD due to the aural similarity.

Ruling
The CJ held that it was possible that aural similarity was enough to create
a likelihood of confusion and the more similar the goods/services covered,
and the more distinctive the earlier mark, the greater the likelihood of confusion.

In determining the distinctive character of a mark and in assessing whether it
is highly distinctive, it is necessary to make a global assessment, taking into
account the visual, aural and conceptual similarities with the earlier mark.
Account should be taken of all relevant factors and, in particular, of the inherent
characteristics of the mark.

The matter is to be judged through the eyes of the average consumer who is
deemed to be reasonably well informed, observant and circumspect. The
level of attention of the average consumer is likely to vary according to the
category of goods in question. Further, the average consumer usually
perceives trade marks in their totality and does not proceed to analyse the
various details.

HÖLTERHOFF

Michael Hölterhoff v Ulrich Freiesleben
C-2/00, 14 May 2002

This decision must be viewed as specific to the facts of this case, where the descriptive reference could in no way be interpreted by the customer as indicating the origin of the product.

Keywords

Infringement & opposition grounds; likelihood of confusion; use of a trade mark for descriptive purposes; Article 5(1) TMD.

Issue

Mr Freiesleben registered the marks SPIRIT SUN and CONTEXT CUT in Germany for diamonds and precious stones. In commercial negotiations Mr Hölterhoff offered for sale to a jeweller semi-precious stones which he described using the names SPIRIT SUN and CONTEXT CUT. The jeweller bought two stones from Mr Hölterhoff in the SPIRIT SUN cut.

Mr Freiesleben successfully sued Mr Hölterhoff for infringement of his German registrations. Mr Hölterhoff appealed and the court referred the matter to the CJ.

Ruling

The CJ ruled that Article 5(1) TMD was to be interpreted as meaning that the proprietor of a trade mark could **not** rely on his exclusive right where the name was solely used to describe the qualities and type of cut of the stones, not to indicate origin.

This ruling is of concern because descriptive use of this nature, if allowed to continue unchallenged, is likely to result in a mark becoming the common name in the trade for the product; a ground for revocation of a registration.

THOMSON LIFE

Medion AG v Thomson Multimedia Sales
Germany & Austria GmbH
C-120/04, 06 October 2005

With composite marks the key question that must now be
answered to establish whether a likelihood of confusion
arises is: Does the earlier mark retain an independent
distinctive role in the composite mark irrespective of
whether or not it is the dominant element? If the answer
to this question is yes, then a likelihood of confusion
(and thus infringement) will have been established.

Keywords

Infringement & opposition grounds; likelihood of confusion; composite marks;
Article 5(1)(b) TMD.

Issue

Medion, the proprietor of a German trade mark for the word LIFE in respect
of electronic devices, objected to Thomson's application for THOMSON LIFE
for identical goods. Medion's case was rejected on the ground that there was
no likelihood of confusion. They appealed and the matter was referred to the CJ.

Ruling

The CJ concluded that there may be a likelihood of confusion where an earlier
sign is taken and juxtaposed with the company name of another where the
earlier sign still retains an independent distinctive role within the composite
mark, even if it is not the most dominant feature.

The CJ decided that despite the fact that the average consumer perceives
a mark as a whole and does not divide it up into its constituent elements,
and even if the overall impression is dominated by one particular element
(THOMSON in THOMSON LIFE), it is still quite possible that the earlier
registered mark can retain an independent distinctive role in the
composite sign.

The use of the composite sign may lead the relevant public to believe that
the goods/services in question derive from companies which are linked,
economically, resulting in a likelihood of confusion.

PICASSO

Claude Ruiz-Picasso, Paloma Ruiz-Picasso,
Maya Widmaier-Picasso, Marina Ruiz-Picasso,
Bernard Ruiz-Picasso v DaimlerChrysler AG & OHIM
C-361/04, 12 January 2006

Since the CJ decision in CANON (page 80), fame
has normally been regarded as tending to increase,
rather than decrease, the ambit of trade mark protection.
This case is an interesting example of fame having the
opposite effect.

Keywords
Infringement & opposition grounds; likelihood of confusion; reputation;
post-sale confusion; average consumer; Article 8(1)(b) CTMR.

Issue
Picasso (who had registered and licensed use of the trade mark PICASSO
to car manufacturer Citroën in respect of vehicles) opposed registration of
the trade mark PICARO by DaimlerChrysler in class 12 on the basis of
a likelihood of confusion. Picasso claimed that because of the fame and
notoriety of Picasso the painter, special protection should be provided to
the trade mark especially because it is highly distinctive. They argued that
in addition to the level of attention of the consumer at the time of purchase,
pre- and post–sale confusion was also relevant.

Ruling
The CJ ruled that greater protection cannot automatically be claimed for
marks with a highly distinctive character when used in a completely different
context to that in which its reputation was earned. In this case, the fame of
the PICASSO name actually created a conceptual difference between the
respective trade marks. The goods had to be taken into consideration. In
respect of motor cars the degree of attention paid by the relevant public at
the time of the purchase is particularly high.

There was no general principle that post-sale confusion was relevant in
determining a likelihood of confusion for Article 8(1)(b) CTMR. Accordingly,
despite a passing similarity (visually and phonetically) between PICASSO
and PICARO this was not felt to be sufficient to give rise to the conclusion
that the purchasing public would believe that the goods came from the
same source.

LEVI STRAUSS

Levi Strauss & Co v Casucci Spa
C-145/05, 27 April 2006

The important date when assessing the alleged
infringement is the date on which the sign was first used.

Keywords
Infringement & opposition grounds; likelihood of confusion; relevant time for
assessing distinctive character; Article 5(1)(b) TMD.

Issue
This case involved overstitching on the rear pocket of pairs
of jeans. Levi had registered what it called the 'seagull'
pocket design in Benelux (above right). Some years
later, Casucci put jeans onto the market in the Benelux
countries bearing a sign comprising a double row of
overstitching, curving upwards in the centre of the back
pockets (below right). Levi brought an action for
trade mark infringement against Casucci seeking cessation
of all use of the mark in question on the clothes marketed by
Casucci and an order for damages against them.

The claim failed at first instance, and on appeal, in part because
the court found that the stitching pattern had ceased to be distinctive.
The issue was referred to the CJ.

Ruling
The CJ said that Article 5(1) TMD must be interpreted as meaning that, when
assessing distinctive character, the national court must take into account the
perception of the public concerned at the date when the alleged infringing
sign was first used rather than the date when the registered mark was first
used.

Further, once infringement has been established it is also for the court to
determine whether, in light of the circumstances prevailing at the time its ruling
is issued, an injunction is an adequate measure to protect the rights in question.
A court may refrain from ordering such a measure if the mark has lost its
disctinctive character in consequence of acts or inactivity of the proprietor.

ADAM OPEL

Adam Opel AG v Autec AG
C-48/05, 25 January 2007

The use of a trade mark as part of a toy replica model
serves only to imitate the original product and is not
trade mark infringement.

Keywords

Infringement & opposition grounds; likelihood of confusion; rights conferred
by a trade mark, honest practices; Article 5(1)(a) TMD; Article 5(2) TMD; Article
6(1)(b) TMD.

Issue

Adam Opel, a motor manufacturer, owned a registration
of a logo (as shown, right) covering, *inter alia*, motor
vehicles and toys. Autec manufactured remote-
controlled scale model cars which they sold under the
name Cartronic. Autec produced a 1:24 remote
controlled scale model of the Opel Astra V8 coupé
bearing the Opel logo as in the original vehicle. Opel applied for an injunction.

The German court referred a number of questions to the CJ, in particular,
"Does use of a logo on toy models of real cars reduced in scale constitute
use of a trade mark for the purposes of Article 5(1)(a) and 5(2)?". If so, "Is the
use an indication of a characteristic of the products as set out in Article 6(1)
(b)" and "What are the criteria to be applied in assessing if this is use in
accordance with honest practices?".

Ruling

The CJ stated that the use in question constituted use of a trade mark but was
not an indication of a characteristic of the scale models. It left it to the German
court to decide whether or not the relevant customers would expect the fixing
of the logo to the model car to be seen as an indication that the car
manufacturer had produced the scale models.

The German District Court decided that the relevant customers of the scale
model would not believe there to be any link between the manufacturer
of the scale model and the car manufacturer. Opel appealed this decision
which was later confirmed by the German Court of Appeal. Opel appealed to
the Federal Supreme Court of Germany who dismissed the appeal (14
January 2010).

TRAVATAN/TRIVASTAN

Alcon Inc v OHIM
C-412/05, 26 April 2007

In establishing whether there is a likelihood of confusion, it is imperatvie to identify who the relevant public is. For pharmaceutical products (even those sold on prescription), the relevant public is likely to comprise healthcare professionals and the end users.

Keywords

Infringement & opposition grounds; likelihood of confusion; relevant public; similarity of marks; Article 8(1)(b) CTMR.

Issue

A CTM application for TRAVATAN for "ophthalmic pharmaceutical products" in class 5 was refused on the basis of a perceived likelihood of confusion with an earlier Italian registration for the mark TRIVASTAN covering "peripheral vasodilator intended to treat ... disorders of the eye and ear" in class 5. The Board of Appeal upheld the Opposition Division's decision and the GC agreed finding significant similarity of the goods and high similarity between the marks.

Ruling

Many pharmaceutical products are only available on prescription given by specialist healthcare professionals and, because of their training and experience, they are unlikely to be confused and so are unlikely to mis-prescribe medicine. However, end users are also aware of brands generally and they rely on a trade mark as an indication of origin. Thus, the GC did not err in law by including end users in the relevant public or err in law by finding that there was a high degree of similarity between the goods in issue for the purposes of applying Article 8(1)(b) CTMR. The CJ also stated that the assessment of similarity of marks depends on, amongst other matters, who is the relevant public. Although the GC did not provide adequate reasons for its assessment of the relevant public by distinguishing between end users and healthcare professionals, this would not invalidate the judgment under appeal.

While patients may be influenced by intermediaries such as healthcare professionals in their choice of a product, this does not preclude a likelihood of confusion amongst patients, nor a finding of similarity. This does not mean that the relevant public for all pharmaceuticals includes end users as some pharmaceutical products are only intended for surgical or hospital use and are not to be sold directly to end users or in pharmacies.

LIMONCELLO

Shaker di L Laudato & C.Sas v Limiñana y Botella, SL
C-334/05, 12 June 2007

The assessment of confusion must take into consideration all elements of the trade mark, including any dominant or distinctive components. However, a dominant figurative element which is different from the earlier mark may not be sufficient to avoid a likelihood of confusion where other elements are similar, even where the elements may be considered descriptive and non-distinctive.

Keywords

Infringement & opposition grounds; likelihood of confusion; global assessment; distinctive and dominant elements; Article 8(1)(b) CTMR.

Issue

Shaker filed a CTM application for a device containing the word LIMONCELLO in respect of lemon liqueurs from the Amalfi Coast in class 33. 'Limoncello' is considered descriptive in Italy for lemon liqueurs from Southern Italy. Limiñana opposed on the basis of its Spanish word mark registration for LIMONCHELO covering alcoholic beverages except beers in class 33.

The Opposition Division and the Board of Appeal found confusion existed on the basis of the similarity of the words LIMONCELLO and LIMONCHELO. The GC held that there was no confusion between the marks as, visually, the dish element in Shaker's mark was the dominant element which was different from the word LIMONCHELO. There was, therefore, no need to consider the phonetic and conceptual similarities between the other elements of the marks.

Ruling

The CJ reiterated that the assessment of confusion must be appreciated globally, based on the overall impression of the marks, bearing in mind their distinctive and dominant elements. The GC did not carry out a global assessment of confusion but focused solely on the dominant element of the marks inferring that, as these were different, it was not necessary to examine any phonetic or conceptual similarities existing between them. As a result, the GC had misapplied Article 8(1)(b) CTMR.

QUICK RESTAURANTS

Société des produits Nestlé SA v OHIM and Quick
Restaurants SA
C-193/06, 20 September 2007

**The distinctiveness of a trade mark must first be assessed
by reference to the goods and services in respect of
which registration is sought and, second, by reference
to the perception of the section of the public targeted.**

Keywords
Infringement & opposition grounds; likelihood of confusion; global
appreciation; distinctive and dominant elements; Article 8(1)(b) CTMR.

Issue
Nestlé applied for a CTM application for the word QUICKY along
with a cartoon figure of a rabbit. Quick Restaurants opposed the
mark based on earlier registrations for the words QUICKIES and
QUICK.

OHIM upheld the opposition on the basis of a likelihood of
confusion. The Board of Appeal and, subsequently, the GC
rejected Nestlé's arguments, maintaining that there was a risk
of confusion.   **QUICKY**

Ruling
The CJ annulled the decision of the GC to the extent that it did not assess
the visual similarity of the signs when relying on the overall impression of
the marks. The figurative element was not dominant and there was only a
conceptual similarity on the basis of the word elements. The assessment
of the similarity between two signs can only be made on the sole dominant
components if all other component of the marks are negligible. The fact that
one element of the sign is not dominant does not imply that it is negligible.

This finding was in line with the assessment in LIMONCELLO (page 89).

MARCA MODE

Adidas AG & Adidas Benelux BV v Marca Mode CV, C&A
Nederland CV, H&M Hennes & Mauritz Netherlands BV &
Vendex KBB Nederland BV
C-102/07, 10 April 2008

The CJ favoured Adidas in this case. Public perception of
an economic link is key, and even use that was intended
to be decorative could infringe.

Keywords

Infringement & opposition grounds; likelihood of confusion; requirement of
availability; scope of protection; economic link; Article 5(1)(b) TMD; Article
5(2) TMD; Article 6(1)(b) TMD.

Issue

Adidas owns a figurative trade mark composed of three vertical stripes of
equal width which are featured on the sides of sports and leisure garments
in a colour which contrasts with the basic colour of those garments. Adidas
brought interlocutory proceedings against a number of third parties to prevent
their use of a two stripe motif on their sports and leisure garments. The third
parties claimed that they were free to use the two stripe motif as this was for
decorative purposes or viewed as an embellishment. The CJ focused on the
extent of Adidas' monopoly rights. The main point at issue was whether
account should be taken of the general public interest in ensuring the availability
of non-distinctive signs was not overly restricted for other traders.

Ruling

The CJ took into account the public interest, in particular the need for
undistorted competition and the concept of free movement of goods and
provision of services. The CJ considered that the two stripe motif was not
obviously a descriptive indication and reiterated that, if the public perceived
the sign as mere decoration, this could negate any likelihood of confusion
for infringement purposes. However if, despite the decorative nature of the
sign, the public is likely to perceive that the goods come from the same or
economically-linked undertakings there would be an infringement of the
earlier right. The CJ reiterated that the more well-known the trade mark,
the greater the number of operators who may want to use similar signs,
consequently diluting the distinctive character of the earlier trade mark.

ARMAFOAM

Armacell Enterprise GmbH v OHIM
C-514/06, 18 September 2008

While CTMs may not be similar in one language, that does not mean that they are not similar in other languages of the EU. From an English speaking practitioner's perspective, this case is particularly relevant for English language marks which may not be similar in English (because they contain some descriptive elements), but may well be similar in another language because their descriptive nature would not be recognised.

Keywords
Infringement & opposition grounds; likelihood of confusion; similarity of marks; language; Article 8(1)(b) CTMR.

Issue
Armacell had applied for a CTM for ARMAFOAM for goods made of elastomers in class 20. This was opposed on the basis of an earlier CTM for NOMAFOAM for similar goods. The Opposition Division rejected the opposition and ruled out a likelihood of confusion. The Board of Appeal subsequently annulled the Opposition Division's decision because, whilst the FOAM element would be understood as quite descriptive for the goods in English, this was not the case for non-English speaking countries. Although the first syllables "AR" and "NO" were different, this was not sufficient to dispel the remaining visual and aural similarities attached to both marks. The GC agreed with the Board of Appeal.

Ruling
The CJ dismissed the appeal in its entirety. It held that it is not necessary for confusion to be likely in all member states of the EU. Confusion in any part of the Community is sufficient to deny protection.

Given the finding that there was likely to be similarity in some non-English speaking countries, the opposition should succeed. This should not, however, prevent the proprietor from seeking to convert its CTM application in the English-speaking countries where there might be no finding of similarity.

The case is important as practitioners must look at the issue of similarity (and indeed likelihood of confusion) from the perspective of all EU languages and not rely solely on their own perceptions of their native tongue.

WATERFORD

Waterford Wedgwood v Assembled Investments
(Proprietary); OHIM
C-398/07, 07 May 2009

As Waterford Wedgwood were able to show that their
trade mark enjoyed a reputation in the UK, an opposition
under Article 8(5) CTMR may have been more likely
to succeed in this case as no similarity between the
corresponding goods/services or likelihood of confusion
is required under this ground.

Keywords

Infringement & opposition grounds; likelihood of confusion; comparison of
goods; Article 8(1)(b) CTMR.

Issue

An application was filed for a figurative trade mark
containing the words WATERFORD STELLENBOSCH
for alcoholic beverages. This was opposed by
Waterford Wedgwood, relying on their earlier rights
in the word mark WATERFORD which was registered

for various articles, including wine glasses, and on the basis that the earlier
mark enjoyed an enhanced reputation. OHIM dismissed the opposition on
both grounds. OHIM's decision was appealed and annulled by the Board of
Appeal. On further appeal the GC annulled the decision of the Board of
Appeal and Waterford Wedgford appealed to the CJ.

Ruling

The CJ dismissed the appeal by Waterford Wedgwood against the GC's
decision that that there was no likelihood of confusion. The CJ confirmed
that a likelihood of confusion was possible, despite a low degree of similarity
between the marks, where the goods and services were very similar and
where the earlier mark was highly distinctive. However, the interdependence
of those factors did not mean that a complete lack of similarity could be fully
offset by the strong distinctive character of the earlier mark. In contrast
to Article 8(5) CTMR, Article 8(1)(b) CTMR provided that the likelihood
of confusion presupposes that the goods/services are identical or
similar. The GC made a detailed assessment of the goods in question
and concluded that although there was a degree of "complementarity"
between glassware and wine, they were not similar. As such, the
necessary condition to establish a likelihood of confusion was lacking.
As the grounds based on Article 8(5) CTMR were not referred to in
the appeal to the CJ, this issue was not considered by them.

CARBONELL

Aceites del Sur-Coosur SA v Koipe Corporación
SL & OHIM
C-498/07, 03 September 2009

The verbal elements of the two trade marks La Española and Carbonell are readily distinguished, but the overall get up of the labels is extremely similar. In a supermarket situation, the courts are often persuaded that the level of attention paid by consumers is not high – they do not read labels.

Keywords
Infringement & opposition grounds; likelihood of confusion; comparison of trade marks; Article 8(1)(b) CTMR.

Issue
The CTM (left image below) was applied for in respect of a range of goods in classes 29 and 30 and was opposed on the basis of an earlier trade mark (right image below) registered in respect of olive oil in class 29.

The Opposition Division initially rejected the opposition on the basis that the signs produced a different overall visual impression. The Board of Appeal agreed. However, the GC overturned the decision, instead finding that the marks were visually similar. The word element 'la Española' was of low distinctive character and did not detract from the overall similarities of the two labels. Consumers may believe that the new product was a sub-brand of the Carbonell product.

Ruling
On further appeal to the CJ, the court confirmed the view of the GC, that the visual comparison was the most important one. Due weight had to be given to the figurative elements of the mark. The average consumer of the relevant goods would not pay a high degree of attention to the marks at the moment of purchase. Consequently the similar visual concept resulted in a likelihood of confusion.

BARBARA BECKER

Barbara Becker v Harman International Industries
Inc & OHIM
C-51/09, 24 June 2010

This is a useful case where arguments need to be
constructed against the common assumption that
surnames possess more of a distinctive character
than forenames.

Keywords
Infringement & opposition grounds; likelihood of confusion; surnames; Article
8(1)(b) CTMR.

Issue
Ms Becker (ex-wife of the former tennis player Boris Becker) filed a CTM
application for the word mark BARBARA BECKER. Harman successfully
opposed this on the basis of two earlier marks containing the element
BECKER (one for BECKER itself). The Board of Appeal annulled this decision.
The GC upheld Harman's challenge to the dismissal of the opposition under
Article 8(1)(b) CTMR. Ms Becker appealed to the CJ.

Ruling
The CJ allowed the appeal, setting aside the decision of the GC. The CJ
said that, although it is possible that in parts of the EU surnames have, as
a general rule, a more distinctive character than forenames, it is appropriate
to take account of factors specific to the case. In particular, the fact that the
surname concerned is unusual or, on the contrary, very common, which is
likely to have an effect on that distinctive character. That was in fact the case
in relation to the common surname 'Becker'.

The CJ also held that the GC had erred in basing its assessment of the
conceptual similarity of the marks on general considerations taken from
the case law without analysing all of the relevant factors specific to the case,
disregarding the requirement of an overall assessment of the likelihood of
confusion based on the overall impression of the marks.

CK

Calvin Klein Trademark Trust v OHIM; Zafra
Marroquineros SL
C-254/09, 02 September 2010

When comparing two marks, similarities between the
dominant elements are key to demonstrating that there
is a likelihood of confusion. In order to succeed in a
reputation claim under Article 8(5) CTMR, the marks
at issue must be identical or at least similar and in this
case they were neither.

Keywords
Infringement & opposition grounds; likelihood of confusion; distinctive and
dominant elements; sub-brands; Article 8(1)(b) CTMR; Article 8(5) CTMR.

Issue
The GC upheld the Board of Appeal decision that there was no likelihood of
confusion under Article 8(1)(b) CTMR between Calvin Klein's CK marks and
the word mark CK CREACIONES KENNYA, applied for by Zafra in relation to
identical goods (clothing and accessories).

The GC held that the overall impression created by the marks differed since
the dominant elements were CK in Calvin Klein's marks and CREACIONES
KENNYA in Zafra's mark. The letters CK were found to occupy an ancillary
position in Zafra's application amounting to a conclusion that the element CK
was negligible. Calvin Klein appealed to the CJ.

Ruling
Calvin Klein could not persuade the CJ that they had a case and the appeal
was dismissed. Their argument that the CK CREACIONES KENNYA mark
would be perceived as one of its sub-brands was rejected and the CJ agreed
with the GC that the marks did not share a common dominant element.

FREE LA LIBERTE N'A PAS DE PRIX

Michalakopoulou Ktimatiki Touristiki AE v OHIM
T-365/09, 27 October 2010

The GC confirmed that it is not a requirement to adjudicate on all grounds put forward in support of an opposition; if an opposition is upheld on the basis of one of the rights relied upon in the opposition, it is not essential to give reasons in respect of any other rights. If no request for proof of use has been made then the comparison of goods must be made on the basis of the specification wording alone and not on the basis of how the mark has been used in practice.

Keywords

Infringement & opposition grounds; likelihood of confusion; examination of earlier rights; comparison of goods/services; Article 8(1)(b) CTMR.

Issue

A CTM application for FREE in respect of goods in class 16 was opposed on the basis of earlier French national word and figurative marks for FREE and FREE LA LIBERTE N'A PAS DE PRIX (image right) in classes 35 and 38. The Opposition  Division rejected the opposition in its entirety but the Board of Appeal upheld the appeal and found a likelihood of confusion under Article 8(1)(b) CTMR. According to the Board of Appeal, there were visual, aural and conceptual similarities between the figurative mark relied upon in the opposition and the mark applied for and some degree of similarity between the goods and services in question. The applicant appealed.

Ruling

Firstly, the GC confirmed that it is necessary to provide reasons in a decision, but the Regulation specifies that OHIM only has to determine whether there is at least one applicable ground for refusing an application. It is not required to adjudicate on all grounds relied upon in an opposition; a decision on the basis of just one of the earlier rights relied upon negates the need for any further discussion on any of the other rights relied upon.

Secondly, a comparison of goods/services must relate to those covered by the registration and not to those for which the earlier mark has been used, unless a request for proof of use has been made and following that, it is apparent that the earlier mark has been used in relation to only part of the goods/services for which it was registered.

FARMA MUNDI

Mundipharma GmbH v OHIM
T-76/09, 22 June 2011

Unless proven otherwise, pharmaceutical goods in class 5 are not complementary to storage, distribution, delivery and packaging services in class 39.

Keywords
Infringement & opposition grounds; likelihood of confusion; complementary goods; Article 8(1)(b) CTMR.

Issue
A CTM application for FARMA MUNDI (figurative) for pharmaceutical preparations in class 5, retailing in class 35 storage, distribution, delivery and packaging in class 39 was opposed on the basis an earlier figurative mark for 'mundi pharma' for pharmaceutical preparations and medical services in classes 5 and 44. A likelihood of confusion was claimed. The Opposition Division upheld the opposition in classes 5 and 35 finding a likelihood of confusion between the marks for these goods and services, but the opposition was rejected for the claimed class 39 services. The Board of Appeal dismissed an appeal in respect of the class 39 finding on the basis that the class 39 services were not similar to any of the goods and services covered by the earlier mark in classes 5 and 44. These goods and services were considered to have a different nature and purpose, were neither interchangeable nor substitutable for one another and were not, therefore, in competition. Furthermore, the class 5 goods and the class 39 services were intended for different target markets (the class 5 goods for end consumers; whereas the class 39 services for professionals).

Mundipharma appealed to the GC on the basis that the Board of Appeal erred in its findings and argued that the class 39 services were complementary as they were inseparable from the pharmaceutical goods in class 5.

Ruling
The GC upheld the Board of Appeal's decision. The manufacture and sale of class 5 goods may involve storage, distribution, delivery and packaging but this connection is not sufficient for them to be considered complementary. Even in the case where a manufacturer of pharmaceuticals also provides packaging and storage, these activities must be considered subsidiary to the manufacturer's main business and not separate from it. The opponent had not provided any evidence to indicate that when a pharmaceutical company provides pharmaceutical products, their transportation and distribution is not part of the usual course of its business activity.

SHOE WITH TWO STRIPES

Adidas AG v OHIM
T-479/08, 29 September 2011

Documents relied on to determine the scope of protection and status of an earlier mark relied on in opposition proceedings must be translated into the language of those proceedings.

Keywords

Infringement & opposition grounds; likelihood of confusion; substantiation of earlier rights; translation; Rule 16(3) Regulation No 2868/95; Rule 17(2) Regulation No 2868/95; Rule 20(2) Regulation No 2868/95.

Issue

Adidas filed an opposition to a figurative sign (below left) based on, *inter alia,* an earlier German trade mark registration (below right). OHIM sent a deficiency notice inviting Adidas to provide a graphic representation of the earlier trade marks and translations into English (language of the proceedings) of the goods forming the basis of the opposition. Adidas filed an extract from the online Register of the German Patent and Trade Mark Office but certain elements were not themselves translated. The Opposition Division upheld the opposition but this was overturned on appeal. The Board of Appeal held that the Opposition Division failed to examine whether the earlier rights were properly substantiated. The partially translated extract could not enable the Board of Appeal to ascertain the existence, validity and scope of the earlier trade mark. Adidas appealed to the GC.

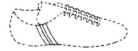 

Ruling

The GC held that only parts of the documents translated into the language of the proceedings are to be taken into consideration. The GC held that the entry corresponding to "type of mark" is vitally important to determine the scope of protection. Similarly, "legal/procedural status" was crucial and covered circumstances such as challenges to the registration and the status of the renewal of the earlier mark. Therefore, a lack of translation in relation to both of these entries meant that it was not possible to deduce the type and validity of the earlier mark. Based on these factors, the GC upheld the Board of Appeal's decision.

ELEPHANTS

Dosenbach-Ochsner AG Schuhe und Sport v OHIM
T-424/10, 07 February 2012

In this case, the GC annulled the contested decision, without full examination as to the merits, due to OHIM's failure to examine a potentially relevant factor in the global assessment of likelihood of confusion. The Board of Appeal failed to appreciate that the proof of use submitted was also intended to support the claim of distinctiveness acquired through use. If the Board of Appeal does not properly consider all of the facts before it the GC cannot properly adjudicate on the legality of decision and must annul it.

Keywords
Infringement & opposition grounds; likelihood of confusion; global assessment; enhanced distinctive character; Article 8(1)(b) CTMR.

Issue
The figurative mark (above right) was registered for a broad range of goods in classes 24 and 25. An invalidity action was brought on the basis of earlier rights in the German word mark 'elephanten' covering shoes and an IR (covering the Czech Republic) and German national right in the figurative mark (below right). The applicant for invalidity claimed a likelihood of confusion under Article 8(1)(b) CTMR. The Cancellation Division dismissed the action on the basis that there was no likelihood of confusion between the contested mark and the earlier rights. The Board of Appeal agreed and the applicant for invalidity appealed to the GC.

Ruling
The Board of Appeal failed to consider the evidence of enhanced distinctive character which the applicant for invalidity claimed for the earlier marks and submitted in the context of proving genuine use. The applicant's submission (claiming enhanced distinctiveness) was sufficiently clear and precise. The evidence submitted was clearly to demonstrate genuine use, as well as acquired distinctiveness. Not to take this evidence into account amounted to a failure to examine a potentially relevant factor in the global assessment of whether there was a likelihood of confusion which consequently rendered the Board of Appeal's decision unsound.

CHEVY

General Motors Corporation v Yplon SA
C-375/97, 14 September 1999

Reputation need only subsist in a member state. However, what constitutes a 'substantial part' is likely to be decided on a case-by-case basis.

Keywords
Infringement & opposition grounds; reputation; Article 5(2) TMD.

Issue
General Motors owned a Benelux registration for the trade mark CHEVY in connection with various goods including motor vehicles. Yplon also owned a Benelux registration for the trade mark CHEVY in connection with detergents and cleaning products in class 3. General Motors sought an injunction restraining Yplon from using the trade mark CHEVY. The question referred to the CJ was firstly what is meant by 'reputation' (as required where there are dissimilar goods/services involved) and, secondly, whether a reputation must exist throughout the Benelux countries or whether it is sufficient for it to exist in part of that territory.

Ruling
The CJ said that a mark enjoys a reputation when it is known by a significant part of the public concerned by the products or services covered by that trade mark. The court must take into consideration all the relevant facts of the case, in particular the market share held by the trade mark, the intensity, the geographical extent and duration of its use, and the size of investment made by the undertaking in promoting it.

Territorially, the condition is fulfilled when the trade mark has a reputation in the member state. In the absence of any definition of the Community provision in this respect, a trade mark cannot be required to have a reputation 'throughout' the territory of the member state. It is sufficient to exist in a substantial part of it.

For the Benelux it is sufficient for a trade mark to have a reputation in a substantial part of the Benelux territory, which may consist of a part of one of the countries composing that territory.

ROBELCO

Robelco NV v Robeco Groep NV
C-23/01, 21 November 2002

Article 5(5) TMD is not a mandatory provision and may be adopted by the member states, at their entire discretion.

Keywords
Infringement & opposition grounds; reputation; Article 5(5) TMD.

Issue
Robeco, a Dutch asset management company, had a Benelux registration for the mark ROBECO. Robeco successfully sued Robelco for trade mark infringement. Robelco appealed that decision to the Court of Appeal in Brussels and questions arose as to the interpretation of Article 5(5) TMD – trade mark infringement by use of a sign other than for the purpose of distinguishing goods/services, for example as a company name. The court was concerned that the provisions of the TMD had not been correctly transposed into Benelux law.

Ruling
The CJ ruled that Article 5(5) TMD is not a mandatory provision and must be interpreted as meaning that a member state may, if it sees fit, and subject to such conditions as it may determine, protect a trade mark against the use of a sign (be it identical or similar to the earlier mark) other than for the purposes of distinguishing goods/services, where use of that sign without due cause takes unfair advantage of, or is detrimental to, the distinctive character or the repute of the trade mark.

DAVIDOFF

Davidoff & Cie SA & Zino Davidoff SA v Gofkid Ltd
C-292/00, 09 January 2003

This case clarifies that the protection afforded to trade marks with a reputation applies to identical and similar goods without a requirement for confusion, where once it was considered that it only extended to dissimilar goods.

Keywords

Infringement & opposition grounds; reputation; protection for identical and similar goods/services; Article 4(4)(a) TMD; Article 5(2) TMD.

Issue

Davidoff uses and owns registrations of the trade mark DAVIDOFF.
Gofkid uses and owns registrations of the trade mark DURFFEE (device).

Davidoff brought proceedings against Gofkid requesting that they stop using the mark and sought annulment of the mark. They argued a likelihood of confusion as Gofkid used the same script as Davidoff. Davidoff alleged that Gofkid was deliberately trying to take advantage of the high-prestige value of the Davidoff mark and to use its advertising appeal. They also claimed that the DURFFEE mark was detrimental to the good reputation of the Davidoff marks. The question referred was whether the registered mark with a reputation is entitled to broader protection where there is no confusion, where the latter mark or sign, which is identical with or similar to the registered mark is intended to be used, or is used, for goods/services identical with those covered by the registered trade mark.

Ruling

The CJ commented that marks with a reputation cannot have less protection, where a sign is used for identical or similar goods/services, than where a sign is used for non-similar goods/services. The TMD is to be interpreted as entitling protection for registered trade marks with a reputation in cases where the conflicting later trade mark or sign is intended to be used or is used for goods/services identical with or similar to those covered by the registered trade mark.

ADIDAS v FITNESSWORLD

Adidas-Salomon AG, Adidas Benelux BV v Fitnessworld
Trading Ltd
C-408/01, 23 October 2003

In practice, in cases of this type, defendants may
find it difficult to establish that there are no trade mark
connotations attached to use of the sign in dispute.
However, for brand owners seeking to enforce their
rights, having to show that use of the sign is not purely
an embellishment and mere decoration is an additional
hurdle to overcome before infringement can be found.

Keywords

Infringement & opposition grounds; reputation; dilution; confusion; unfair
advantage; use as a trade mark; decoration; Article 5(2) TMD.

Issue

Adidas, the owner of the well-known three stripe trade mark, sued Fitnessworld
for infringement in the Netherlands claiming that their use of two stripes would
cause confusion and that such use took unfair advantage of its well-known
three striped mark. On appeal the Dutch court found that customers would
not be confused as Fitnessworld were only using their two stripe motif for
embellishment or decoration. The Dutch Supreme Court listened to arguments
from Adidas that it should enjoy an enhanced protection following DAVIDOFF
(page 103) before referring questions to the CJ including whether
infringement would arise even where the public would only view the signs
as being a decoration rather than trade mark use.

Ruling

Not surprisingly, following DAVIDOFF the CJ reaffirmed its judgment that
protection exists for marks even without a finding of confusion, as long as
a link could be established between the offending sign and the mark with
a reputation.

On the second point, the CJ held that where a sign is viewed as an
embellishment or decoration, this would not necessarily be an obstacle
to the protection given by Article 5(2) TMD, as long as the public establish a
link between the sign and the mark. If the sign is viewed purely as an
embellishment and no link is established as a matter of fact, Article 5(2)
TMD does not apply.

INTEL

Intel Corporation Inc v CPM United Kingdom Ltd
C-252/07, 27 November 2008

The requirements for infringement of a mark with a reputation by a similar mark used on dissimilar goods/ services cannot be listed exhaustively. The assessment must be global, taking all relevant facts into consideration.

Keywords
Infringement & opposition grounds; reputation; dilution; unfair advantage; detriment; Article 4(4)(a) TMD.

Issue
Intel unsuccessfully applied to invalidate the trade mark INTELMARK in the UK in respect of marketing and telemarketing services in class 35. The court noted that the INTEL mark is 'unique' in a sense that it is not used by anyone else, and that Intel has a huge reputation in the UK for computers and computer linked products. According to the UKIPO and EWHC, Intel had not shown either detriment to the distinctive character of the INTEL trade mark or the repute thereof, or that an unfair advantage of Intel's rights had been taken by the owners of the INTELMARK trade mark. Intel appealed to the Court of Appeal, which referred the case to the CJ.

Ruling
The CJ concluded, that for the average consumer, if the later mark called the earlier mark with a reputation to mind, then this is tantamount to the existence of a link – a preliminary requirement for a finding of dilution. The CJ noted, however, that merely because the earlier mark has a huge reputation and that the earlier mark is unique in respect of any goods and services, does not necessarily imply that there is a link between the conflicting marks or establish unfair advantage or detriment. The court must take into account all factors relevant to the case to establish the existence of a link, unfair advantage or detriment.

The CJ also stated that establishing 'detriment to distinctiveness' does not necessarily involve economic detriment. Therefore a change in economic behaviour is not essential.

TDK

Aktieselskabet af 21 November 2001 v TDK Corp
C-197/07, 12 December 2008

For a claim under Article 8(5) CTMR, it is sufficient to show that a 'risk' of unfair advantage or detriment would likely be caused in the future, provided that some link can be established, past or present, between the goods or services and the earlier mark.

Keywords
Infringement & opposition grounds; reputation; unfair advantage; detriment; economic link; Article 8(5) CTMR.

Issue
Aktieselskabet filed a CTM application for the mark TDK in relation to clothing, footwear and headgear. TDK Corp opposed under Article 8(1)(b) CTMR and Article 8(5) CTMR on the basis of earlier marks registered in relation to apparatus for recording transmission or reproduction of sound or images.

The GC, comparing the two TDK marks, allowed the opposition under Article 8(5) CTMR concluding that following INTEL (page 106), it was not necessary to demonstrate actual and present injury to an earlier mark; it was sufficient to show that there was a risk of unfair advantage or detriment in the future.

Ruling
The CJ dismissed the appeal from the GC decision holding that the earlier mark had a reputation and a link would be made between the goods because TDK's mark had been used in the past on clothing for sponsorship.

NASDAQ

Antartica Srl v OHIM (defendant at first instance) &
The Nasdaq Stock Market Inc (intervener at first instance)
C-320/07, 12 March 2009

The fact that a reputation can be gained even in respect
of services that are offered for free is an interesting
development.

Keywords
Infringement & opposition grounds; reputation; relevant public; Article 8(5)
CTMR.

Issue
Antartica applied to register the trade mark
NASDAQ (stylised). Their application was
opposed by The Nasdaq Stock Market, Inc
(NASDAQ) on the basis of their earlier CTM for

NASDAQ. This opposition was rejected on the grounds that the reputation of
NASDAQ had not been properly substantiated. An appeal followed and the
Board of Appeal reversed OHIM's decision, finding that the reputation of
NASDAQ for services in classes 35 and 36 had been substantiated.
Antartica appealed to the GC which upheld the Board of Appeal's decision.
In further appealing the case to the CJ, Antartica claimed that:

○ use of the mark is established only if it is used in connection with the sale
of goods/services. In this case, NASDAQ indices were available free of
charge and no evidence had been adduced to the effect that those indices
are for sale within the Community; and
○ consumers of the goods covered by the trade mark applied for are not
aware of the earlier mark and, therefore, contrary to the view of the GC,
unfair advantage can be ruled out.

Ruling
The CJ found that even when part of the services are offered free of charge,
it does not mean that the commercial company will not seek to create or
maintain an outlet for those services. It reiterated its findings in INTEL
(page 106) and said that the existence of a link must be subject to an overall
assessment, taking into account all factors of the case. Antartica's argument
relating to the relevant public was rejected as unfounded.

PAGO

PAGO International GmbH v Tirolmilch registrierte GmbH
C-301/07, 06 October 2009

The decision highlights the scope of protection afforded to brand owners of a CTM who trade in only one member state. However, it remains unclear whether a CTM with a reputation in only part of a member state is sufficient.

Keywords
Infringement & opposition grounds; reputation; Article 9(1)(c) CTMR.

Issue
Pago owned a CTM registration for fruit drinks and fruit juices consisting of a green glass bottle with a distinctive label and cap next to a full glass of fruit drink. Tirol sold a drink called 'Lattella' in glass bottles which resembled (in shape, colour, label and cap) the bottle depicted in Pago's CTM. Tirol used a representation of a bottle next to a full glass in advertising, much like Pago's CTM.

Pago brought proceedings in Austria against Tirol and the court referred to the CJ the question of the meaning of 'reputation in the Community' under Article 9(1)(c) CTMR and whether a reputation in only one member state is sufficient.

Ruling
The CJ ruled that 'reputation in the Community' means that the CTM must be known by a significant part of the public concerned by the products or services covered by the CTM in a substantial part of the Community. This follows the line taken in CHEVY (page 101). What constitutes a substantial part of the Community is not dependent on national boundaries but must be determined by an assessment of all the relevant circumstances.

On the facts of the case, one member state could constitute a substantial part of the Community. It was therefore enough for Pago to show that their CTM was known throughout Austria.

KINDER

Ferrero SpA v OHIM
C-552/09, 24 March 2011

No matter how great the reputation of an earlier mark, if the earlier mark and the opposed mark are not similar, the public will make no link between them sufficient to invoke Article 8(5) of the CTMR. This will be the case even if the earlier mark is one of a large family of similar marks.

Keywords

Infringement & opposition grounds; reputation; family of marks; Article 8(5) CTMR.

Issue

Ferrero is the owner of the KINDER family of marks, which has a significant reputation in the EU for chocolate confectionery in particular. The applicant had applied for a  figurative CTM (above right) for TIMI KINDERJOGHURT for a range of yogurt products. Ferrero opposed, but lost. Ferrero then sought invalidation of the registered CTM on the basis of, *inter alia*, Article 8(5) CTMR. The action was upheld by the Cancellation Division but overturned on appeal because the Board of Appeal said it was bound to the findings made in the opposition proceedings. On appeal, the GC said, *obiter*, that the Board of Appeal was wrong to hold that it was bound in invalidity proceedings by findings made in a final decision in opposition proceedings. As this was not pleaded, the GC could not comment further or uphold the appeal on that fact alone. The GC confirmed that the action was unfounded because the marks are not similar and similarity is a precondition for Article 8(1)(b) CTMR and Article 8(5) CTMR.

Ruling

The appeal was dismissed. The CJ found that the GC was correct in deciding that, if the marks were not considered similar, there would be no link perceived by the public (no matter how great the reputation). Whilst reputation was relevant to ascertaining whether the relevant public makes a link, if the marks are not, in fact, similar, reputation cannot affect that finding. Without similarity, Article 8(5) CTMR cannot be invoked.

Even if the earlier mark was part of a large family of marks, if there is insufficient similarity, then there would be no link.

GOOGLE v LOUIS VUITTON

Google France SARL, Google Inc v Louis Vuitton
Malletier SA & Others
Joined cases C-236/08 to C-238/08, 23 March 2010

AdWords are a significant part of Google's business, and
a finding that they helped infringe third party trade mark
rights by offering AdWords for sale would have been a
significant blow to Google. However, the CJ found that
brand owners would have the right to prevent use of their
trade marks in AdWords only where that use resulted in
confusion as to the origin of the goods/services.

Keywords
Infringement & opposition grounds; keywords; AdWords; Article 5(1) TMD;
Article 5(2) TMD; Article 9 CTMR.

Issue
Google operates an AdWords system which allows advertisers to purchase
competitors' trade marks as keywords, in order to trigger sponsored links in
internet search results.

Ruling
The CJ found that Google's AdWords system does not infringe the trade mark
rights of a brand owner when the brand owner's marks are used by another to
trigger sponsored adverts. The CJ found that Google's role was only that of
an internet referencing service provider and Google did not itself violate any
trade mark rights.

Where third party advertisements suggest that there is an economic link
between that third party and the proprietor of the trade mark, the conclusion
must be that there is an adverse effect on the origin function, and infringement
is possible.

PORTAKABIN

Portakabin Limited and Portakabin BV v Primakabin BV
C 558/08, 08 July 2010

The ruling provides some level of comfort to trade mark owners whose trade marks are being used in adverts without their consent, but unless there are legitimate reasons to prohibit the advert, trade mark owners may find it difficult to challenge adverts where the goods are already available in the EEA with the proprietor's consent.

Keywords

Infringement & opposition grounds; keywords; AdWords; Article 5 TMD; Article 6 TMD; Article 7 TMD.

Issue

Primakabin sold various mobile building structures, including those made by Portakabin and used the PORTAKABIN trade mark in an internet advert for 'used portakabins'. Portakabin sued for infringement and although Portakabin were partially successful on appeal, they appealed to the Supreme Court in the Netherlands to determine whether use of PORTAKABIN in adverts amounted to use of the mark for goods/services. This was referred to the CJ.

Ruling

The CJ held that an advert that uses an identical or similar trade mark, without the consent of the proprietor, can be prohibited if consumers cannot identify the origin of the goods/services, but it will be for national courts to assess whether use is in accordance with honest practices. A proprietor cannot prevent advertisers from advertising the resale of goods if those goods have already been put on the market in the EEA with the proprietor's consent, unless there is a legitimate reason to do so. A legitimate reason to prohibit the advert must be found where the reseller, without the proprietor's consent, removes all references to the trade mark from goods already placed on the market and replaces these with the reseller's name. Specialist resellers of second hand goods cannot be prohibited from using another's trade mark to advertise the goods to the public unless there is a risk of damage to the trade mark. National courts cannot prohibit adverts merely on the basis that they use words such as 'second hand' or 'used'.

INTERFLORA

Interflora Inc & Other v Marks & Spencer plc (M&S) & Other
C-323/09, 22 September 2011

Internet keywords that are identical to earlier registered marks and used in respect of identical goods/services may infringe where the origin, advertising and investment functions of the mark are adversely affected. Owners of marks with a reputation may prevent use of keywords if it amounts to free-riding, dilution or tarnishment of the distinctive character or repute of the mark.

Keywords

Infringement & opposition grounds; keywords; keyword advertising; essential function; reputation; free-riding; tarnishment; dilution; Article 5(1)(a) TMD; Article 5(2) TMD; Article 9(1)(a) & (c) CTMR.

Issue

M&S had purchased the term 'Interflora' (identical to Interflora's trade mark) to promote its flower delivery service. Where 'Interflora' was searched as a term, an advertisement for M&S's flower service was displayed in the form of a sponsored link. Interflora sued for trade mark infringement and the English court referred questions to the CJ: Is the proprietor of a mark entitled to prevent a competitor from displaying an advertisement, by way of an Internet referencing service constituting a sign which is identical to its mark and relates to identical goods/services without consent? In those circumstances, is it relevant if the advertisement is liable to mislead the relevant public and the mark has a reputation?

Ruling

A trade mark proprietor is entitled to prevent the use of a keyword where it is identical to their mark and used in relation to identical goods/services if that use adversely affects one of the mark's functions. Such use adversely affects the origin function if the advertisement displayed means reasonably well-informed or observant Internet users cannot (or only with difficulty) ascertain whether advertised goods/services emanate from the mark owner or a third party. Such use does not adversely affect the advertising function, but does adversely affect the investment function if it substantially interferes with the proprietor's use of its mark to acquire or preserve a reputation.

For marks with a reputation the owner may object where the keyword purchaser thereby takes an unfair advantage of or causes detriment to the mark's distinctive character or repute (for example, generic use). However, merely offering an alternative to the goods/services of the mark's proprietor is acceptable.

O2 v HUTCHISON 3G

O2 Holdings Ltd & O2 UK Ltd v Hutchison 3G UK Ltd
C-533/06, 12 June 2008

If there was no confusion, there can be no infringement. It was accepted that the advertisement had not given rise to a likelihood of confusion.

Keywords

Infringement & opposition grounds; comparative advertising; likelihood of confusion; Article 5(1) TMD; Article 3a(1) CAD.

Issue

Hutchison 3G used bubble imagery in comparative advertisements which were similar to registered bubble device trade marks held by O2. The Court of Appeal referred three questions to the CJ for clarification, regarding:

○ whether the use fell within Article 5(1) TMD;
○ whether that use must be indispensable in order to comply with the CAD, and if so;
○ what are the criteria by which such indispensability is to be judged?

Under Article 5(1) TMD, the owner of a registered trade mark is entitled to prevent third parties from using in the course of trade any sign identical/similar to the trade mark in relation to identical/similar goods/services, where there exists a likelihood of confusion on the part of the public. Hutchison argued that their use fell within the defences for infringement in the TMD if it complied with the CAD. O2 claimed that the bubbles were not used descriptively and were used as a way of describing Hutchison's own services by comparing them with those of O2. O2 also argued that the terms of the CAD included a requirement of necessity, ie, that the trade mark was indispensable to the advert, otherwise using the third party trade mark would take unfair advantage of that trade mark.

Ruling

The CJ said that it was not necessary for the comparative advert to use the competitor's exact trade mark, use of a similar sign was permissible. The court also held that it was necessary to reconcile the TMD and the CAD. A proprietor was not entitled to prevent the use by a third party of a sign identical or similar to the proprietor's mark in comparative advertising where all the conditions laid down in the CAD were satisfied, unless the requirements of Article 5(1) TMD were satisfied. In this case, as there was no likelihood of confusion established, O2 was unsuccessful.

L'ORÉAL v BELLURE

L'Oréal SA & Others v Bellure NV & Others
C-487/07, 18 June 2009

This decision should help to protect brand owners against 'look-a-likes'. The concept of unfair advantage clearly focuses on benefit to the third party user, rather than on harm to the well-known mark. It recognises that trade marks have functions other than as an indicator of origin. They may be a symbol of exclusivity and prestige, and the proprietor's marketing investment in such brands deserves protection.

Keywords
Infringement & opposition grounds; comparative advertising; look-a-likes; without due cause; Article 5(1) TMD; Article 5(2) TMD.

Issue
Bellure packaged and branded perfumes in a way designed to evoke the TRESOR and MIRACLE products and had promoted their perfumes through comparative price lists. Bellure's witness admitted the choice of packaging and branding was deliberate. L'Oréal alleged Bellure's actions were taken without due cause and took unfair advantage of their marks. The UK Court of Appeal requested the CJ's ruling on whether the use of the packaging/branding constituted infringement in the absence of demonstrable confusion on the part of the purchaser and whether the references in the price lists constituted infringement if the references did not jeopardise the essential function of the trade mark as an indication of origin.

Ruling
In view of Bellure's admission, the CJ did not need to consider whether they had acted without due cause. The CJ reaffirmed that the trade mark owner has a right to a level of protection which will ensure that the mark can fulfil its functions, which include its function not only as a guarantee of origin and quality but also extends to its investment or advertising. Bellure compared its products unfairly with L'Oréal and also sought to advertise its goods by 'riding on L'Oréal's coat-tails', which was not viewed as fair use.

BMW

Bayerische Motorenwerke AG (BMW) & BMW Nederland
BV v Ronald Karel Deenik
C-63/97, 23 February 1999

This case confirms that it is permissible for a third
party to use another's trade mark where it is necessary
for the purposes of advertising the nature of their goods/
services. However, such use must be factual and should
not suggest any relationship between the two entities.

Keywords

Infringement & opposition grounds; defences to infringement; necessary
to indicate intended purpose; honest use; Article 5 TMD; Article 6 TMD;
Article 7 TMD.

Issue

Mr Deenik was an independent garage owner specialising in the sale, repair
and maintenance of second hand BMW cars and used the BMW trade mark
in the course of advertising his services. He was not a member of BMW's
authorised dealer network. The question referred to the CJ related to whether
an independent garage selling and repairing BMW cars had the right to use
expressions such as 'repair and maintenance of BMWs' and 'BMW specialist'.

Ruling

The CJ said that Deenik was able to use such expressions. It was not for
BMW to decide who was entitled to describe themselves as such a specialist.
However, the CJ noted that if the defendant used the BMW trade mark to
create the impression that he was affiliated to BMW's distribution network,
then the use would fall foul of the honesty requirement (see GILLETTE,
page 121) and would be an infringement.

GERRI v KERRY SPRING

Gerolsteiner Brunnen GmbH & Co v Putsch GmbH
C-100/02, 07 January 2004

This case illustrates the particular difficulty that arises
where there are conflicts between trade marks and
geographical indications. Where a geographical indication
is used in accordance with honest practices, such use
cannot be prevented even where it is similar to an earlier
registered trade mark and a national court finds that there
is a likelihood of confusion.

Keywords
Infringement & opposition grounds; defences to infringement; geographical
indications; Article 6(1)(b) TMD.

Issue
Gerolsteiner owns the trade mark GERRI and commenced infringement
proceedings in Germany against a marketing and distribution company,
Putsch, for offering for sale imported mineral water under the brand KERRY
SPRING. The defendant's goods are produced by The Kerry Company
in Ireland using water from a spring known as Kerry Spring.

The German courts had no hesitation in concluding that the marks were
similar on the basis that there was a likelihood of aural confusion. The case
was referred to the CJ, as the German Supreme Court was unsure as to
whether a finding for infringement should be made, given that KERRY
SPRING is an indication of geographical origin and was being used in
accordance with honest practices.

Ruling
The CJ very clearly set out that if the defendant's mark is a geographical
term, and would be viewed as such, use of the geographical indication
cannot be prevented by the owner of the earlier registered trade mark,
despite potential confusion. The CJ declined to apply its guidelines in
principle to the specific facts of the case, leaving this overall assessment
to the national court.

GILLETTE

The Gillette Company & Gillette Group Finland Oy v LA-Laboratories Ltd Oy
C-228/03, 17 March 2005

Brand owners cannot object to third party use of their trade marks where it is necessary to indicate the intended purpose of the goods, provided that such use is in accordance with honest practices, as this would distort the system of competition in the market for replacement products or spare parts.

Keywords

Infringement & opposition grounds; defences to infringement; necessary to indicate intended purpose; honest use; Article 6(1)(c) TMD.

Issue

LA-Laboratories produced replacement razor blades designed to fit third party branded products. The packaging contained the wording: "All handles of Parason Flexor and Gillette Sensor are compatible with this blade." The legality of this was referred to the CJ.

Ruling

The CJ found that use of a third party trade mark is permissible if it is necessary to indicate the intended purpose of the goods, provided that such use is in accordance with honest practices in industrial or commercial matters. Such use must not suggest a commercial link between the parties and must not affect the value of the trade mark by taking unfair advantage of its distinctive character or by denigrating or discrediting the mark. The third party product must not be presented as a replica or imitation of the branded product.

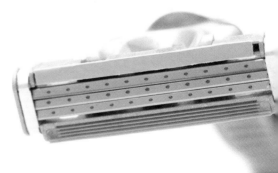

RED BULL v WINTERS

Frisdranken Industrie Winters BV v Red Bull GmbH
C-119/10, 15 December 2011

It is not 'use in the course of trade' for a company to fill packaging under instructions from a third party, who in advance affixed to the packaging a sign which is identical or similar to a sign protected as a trade mark.

Keywords

Infringement & opposition grounds; use of a sign in the course of trade; filling of cans; Article 5(1) & (3) TMD.

Issue

Red Bull instituted interlocutory proceedings in the Benelux to prevent Winters, a company specialising in filling cans with drinks, from filling empty cans bearing various signs that Red Bull considered to infringe its trade marks. Winters received its instructions to fill the cans and the cans themselves bearing the potentially infringing signs from Smart Drinks Ltd, a competitor of Red Bull. The signs included BULLFIGHTER, PITTBULL, RED HORN, LONG HORN and LIVE WIRE.

The District Court found that Winters' filling of the cans must be deemed 'use in the course of trade' and that there was similarity with respect to the BULLFIGHTER mark only. Both parties appealed. The Court of Appeal agreed with the first decision but also considered that there was similarity with respect to the signs PITTBULL and LIVE WIRE. Red Bull appealed again to the Supreme Court who referred questions to the CJ to find out if the mere 'filling' of packaging, to which a sign has been affixed by another party, is to be regarded as use in the course of trade.

Ruling

The CJ held that Winters does not itself 'use' the sign applied to the cans by merely filling those cans upon instructions from another party. Winters is simply executing a technical part of the production process. Furthermore, the service of filling cans is not similar to the product in relation to which Red Bull has registered its trade marks. The consumer will not, therefore, be aware of the party who undertakes the filling of the cans so that there is no link between the sign and the filling service.

D YOUNG&CO
EXHAUSTION OF RIGHTS & PARALLEL IMPORTS

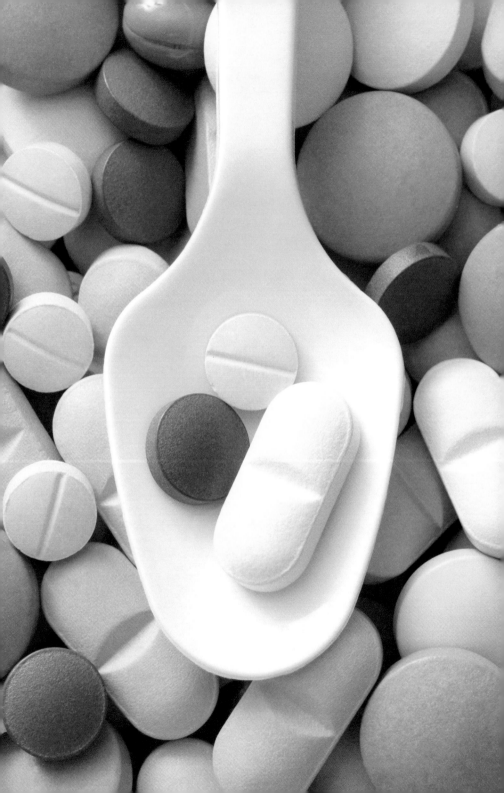

PARANOVA

Bristol-Myers Squibb v Paranova A/S; C H Boehringer Sohn,
Boehringer Ingelheim KG & Boehringer Ingelheim AS
v Paranova A/S; Bayer Aktiengesellschaft & Bayer Danmark
A/S v Paranova A/S
Joined cases C-427/93, C-429/93 & C-436/93, 11 July 1996

The test of 'necessity' is interpreted widely. Repackaging
is considered necessary where effective access to the
market concerned would otherwise be hindered, for
example where the products would otherwise be viewed
less favourably by consumers (see MSD v PARANOVA,
page 134).

Keywords

Exhaustion of rights & parallel imports; repackaging; Article 7 TMD; Article 30
TFEU; Article 36 TFEU.

Issue

Paranova imported medicines from Greece and other EU countries where
the prices were low and sold them at a profit in Denmark. The medicines
had been repackaged with new outer packaging/labels appropriate for sale
in Denmark.

Ruling

A trade mark owner cannot oppose the marketing of repackaged products
where the following five conditions have been met:

○ Reliance on the trade mark to oppose the parallel import would lead to
'artificial partitioning' of the single market.
○ The repackaging does not directly or indirectly affect the original condition
of the product.
○ The new packaging clearly indicates the name of the original trade mark
owner and the repackager.
○ The new packaging is not liable to damage the reputation of the trade
mark or its owner.
○ The repackager declares the repackaging activity to the original owner
and, upon request, presents a sample to the original owner.

Where the above conditions have been met and the product's reputation is
not prejudiced by the repackaging, a trade mark owner will not be able to
object to the activity. However, such repackaging is permissible only to the
extent that this is necessary for the product to be marketed in another country.

DIOR v EVORA

Parfums Christian Dior SA & BV v Evora BV
C-337/95, 04 November 1997

The CJ recognised a new type of damage to the condition
of the trade marked goods: damage to the prestigious
image or luxurious aura of the goods. However, such
damage must be serious to provide a defence against
the exhaustion of rights principle.

Keywords
Exhaustion of rights & parallel imports; damage to aura of luxury; Article 5
TMD; Article 7 TMD; Article 30 TFEU; Article 36 TFEU.

Issue
Evora operated a chain of chemist shops. As part of a Christmas promotion,
Evora produced an advertising leaflet which featured pictures of (lawfully
parallel imported) Dior trade marked perfumes POISON, DUNE, FARENHEIT
and EAU SAUVAGE. Dior claimed trade mark infringement, complaining that
such advertising detracted from the luxurious and prestigious image of the
registered marks.

Ruling
The CJ found that when trade marked goods have been put on the market
in the Community by the trade mark proprietor, or with the trade mark
proprietor's consent, a reseller, besides being free to resell those goods,
is also free to make use of the trade mark, in order to bring to the public's
attention the further commercialisation of those goods. Thus the proprietor's
trade mark rights are exhausted. However, the exhaustion of rights rule does
not apply where there are legitimate reasons for the proprietor to oppose
further commercialisation of trade marked goods, especially where the
condition of the goods is changed or impaired after they have been put
on the market. Damage to the reputation of a mark could be such a legitimate
reason. The defendant must take steps to prevent its advertising from affecting
the value of the trade mark by detracting from the allure and prestigious
image of the goods and their aura of luxury.

SILHOUETTE

Silhouette International Schmied GmbH & Co KG
v Hartlauer Handelsgesellschaft mbH
C-355/96, 16 July 1998

At the time this case was particularly groundbreaking, signalling a 'fortress Europe' in terms of trade mark rights. The correct approach was considered to be Community-wide exhaustion of rights.

Keywords
Exhaustion of rights & parallel imports; Community exhaustion; Article 7 TMD.

Issue
Hartlauer imported genuine but discontinued lines of SILHOUETTE branded spectacle frames from Bulgaria (outside the EEA at the time) into the EU (specifically Austria). Silhouette claimed infringement of their Austrian SILHOUETTE trade mark rights.

Ruling
The CJ ruled that there was no principle of international exhaustion of rights. Trade mark rights are only exhausted where the trade marked goods have been put on the market within the EEA by the trade mark proprietor or with the trade mark proprietor's consent. Therefore the correct approach is Community-wide exhaustion of rights. Each specific batch of goods must have been put on the market in the EEA by the trade mark proprietor or with the trade mark proprietor's consent in order for the exhaustion principle to apply.

SEBAGO

Sebago Inc & Ancienne Maison Dubois et Fils SA
v GB-Unic SA
C-173/98, 01 July 1999

Each individual item must be put on the market in the EEA by the trade mark proprietor, or with the trade mark proprietor's consent, in order for the exhaustion principle to apply.

Keywords

Exhaustion of rights & parallel imports; consent; Article 7(1) TMD.

Issue

GB-Unic sold dockside shoes which were genuine but imported from outside the EEA.

Once trade marked goods have been put on the market in the EEA by the trade mark proprietor, or with the trade mark proprietor's consent, trade mark rights are exhausted. That is, trade mark proprietors cannot rely on their rights to oppose further commercialisation of the goods.

The issue of the definition of 'consent' in this context was referred to the CJ.

Ruling

The CJ held that consent must relate to each individual item of the product in respect of which exhaustion is pleaded. Trade mark rights were not exhausted simply by the proprietor consenting to the use of the mark on other goods in the EEA (even if such goods were identical to those in issue).

UPJOHN

Pharmacia & Upjohn SA v Paranova A/S
C-379/97, 12 October 1999

Subsequent cases have interpreted the requirement
to be 'objectively necessary' widely. Repackaging is
considered necessary where effective access to the
market concerned would otherwise be hindered, for
example, where the products would alternatively be
viewed less favourably by consumers, (see MSD v
PARANOVA, page 134).

Keywords
Exhaustion of rights & parallel imports; repackaging of products; Article 7
TMD.

Issue
Upjohn marketed antibiotics throughout the EU under the trade marks
DALACIN, DALACINE and DALACIN C. Different versions of the brand
were used in different countries. Paranova bought the products in one
country where they were packaged under one brand and repackaged
them to be suitable for sale in another country (under the brand used there).

Ruling
The CJ held that such repackaging is only allowed if it is 'objectively necessary'
for the parallel importer to be able to put the product on the market in
another country.

This condition is satisfied if, by not replacing the mark, effective access to
the market of the importing member state would be hindered. However, the
condition will not be satisfied if replacement of the mark can be explained
solely as an attempt by the parallel importer to secure a commercial advantage.

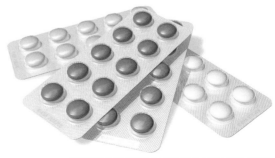

DAVIDOFF & LEVI

Zino Davidoff SA v A&G Imports Ltd; Levi Strauss & Co/Levi Strauss (UK) Ltd v Tesco Stores Ltd/Tesco plc; Levi Strauss & Co/Levi Strauss (UK) Ltd v Costco Wholesale UK Ltd
Joined cases C-414/99 to C-416/99, 20 November 2001

A trade mark proprietor's rights are not exhausted unless the goods have been put on on the market in the EEA directly, or with the trade mark proprietor's consent. Although consent can be implied from the circumstances, it must be 'unequivocal'.

Keywords
Exhaustion of rights & parallel imports; infringement; consent to marketing in the EEA; Article 5 TMD; Article 7(1) TMD.

Issue
In the first action Davidoff entered into an exclusive distribution contract with a trader in Singapore, for products bearing its trade marks COOL WATER and DAVIDOFF COOL WATER. The distributor undertook to sell the products within a defined territory outside the EEA and to impose a prohibition of resale upon its local sub-distributors. A&G obtained stocks of the products, removed the batch code and imported the products into the UK.

In the other actions, Levi refused to sell their Levi's 501 jeans to Tesco and Costco. Tesco and Costco obtained the jeans from countries outside the EEA, imported them, and sold them in the UK. The suppliers outside the EEA were under contractual restrictions prohibiting resale to wholesalers or for export. The questions referred to the CJ concerned the nature of the consent required from a registered proprietor to market its products in the EEA.

Ruling
The CJ held that consent had to unequivocally demonstrate an intention to renounce those rights. This could be an express statement, but in some cases could be implied. The onus was on the trader to show that consent had been given. Implied consent could not be inferred from silence of the proprietor; nor from the failure of the goods to carry any warning that their marketing in the EEA was prohibited or the fact that the proprietor had not placed any express contractual restrictions on the resale of the goods in the EEA.

It is not relevant that the importer may not be aware that the proprietor objects to those goods being sold in the EEA or that an authorised seller has not imposed contractual restrictions on their own purchasers.

BOEHRINGER

Boehringer Ingelheim KG/Boehringer Ingelheim Pharma KG; Glaxo Group Ltd; The Wellcome Foundation Ltd; SmithKline Beecham plc/Beecham Group plc/SmithKline & French Laboratories Ltd; Eli Lilly & Co v Dowelhurst Ltd & Swingward Ltd
C-143/00, 23 April 2002

Following the decision in PARANOVA (page 127) issued by the CJ in 1996, the criteria on repackaging of parallel imported products has been relatively clear. Subsequent cases have attempted to further define (and limit) those criteria with little success. The fundamental principle of EU law remains that trade mark rights cannot be used to artificially partition the market and where the 'Paranova criteria' have been met, repackaging will be allowed.

Keywords
Exhaustion of rights & parallel imports; repackaging; requirement to give notice; Article 7(2) TMD.

Issue
In the cases of PARANOVA (page 127), the CJ established the criteria which a parallel importer who chooses to repackage branded products must meet to avoid objection from trade mark owners. These criteria include a requirement to give notice of the intended repackaging to the trade mark proprietor.

Ruling
In this case, the CJ held that notice must be given to the trade mark proprietor by the parallel importer himself and, in the event of a dispute regarding notice, it is for the national court charged with the case to assess whether, in all the circumstances, the trade mark proprietor had a reasonable time to react to the intended repackaging.

MSD v PARANOVA

Merck, Sharp & Dohme GmbH
v Paranova Pharmazeutika Handels GmbH
C-443/99, 23 April 2002

Following the decision in PARANOVA (page 127) issued
by the CJ in 1996, the law on repackaging of parallel
imported products has been relatively clear. Subsequent
cases brought by trade mark proprietors have attempted
to further define (and limit) those criteria such as the
definition of 'necessity', with little success. The
fundamental principle of EU law remains that trade
mark rights cannot be used to artificially partition the
market and where the Paranova criteria have been met,
repackaging will be allowed.

Keywords
Exhaustion of rights & parallel imports; repackaging; necessity; Article 7(2) TMD.

Issue
In the cases of PARANOVA (page 127), the CJ established the criteria which
a parallel importer who chooses to repackage branded products must meet
to avoid objection from trade mark owners. These criteria include a
requirement that the repackaging is necessary for the product to be marketed
in the new country.

Ruling
In this case, the CJ held that "replacement packaging of pharmaceutical
products is objectively necessary within the meaning of the court's case
law if, without such repackaging, effective access to the market concerned,
or to a substantial part of that market, must be considered to be hindered as
the result of strong resistance from a significant proportion of consumers to
relabelled pharmaceutical products."

VAN DOREN

Van Doren & Q GmbH v Lifestyle Sports & Sportswear Handelsgesellschaft mbH
C-244/00, 08 April 2003

If a party wishes to avail itself of a defence to infringement, it should be for that party to show that the requirements of the defence exist.

Keywords
Exhaustion of rights & parallel imports; burden of proof; Article 7 TMD.

Issue
Van Doren was the exclusive importer of STÜSSY branded goods in the EEA. A third party began importing clothing bearing the trade mark STÜSSY.

Ruling
If the clothing had actually been obtained from elsewhere in the EEA, trade mark rights would be exhausted. If parallel importers want to rely on the defence of exhaustion of rights, they must prove that the goods originated inside the EEA (or that the trade mark proprietor has consented to their marketing in the EEA) and that infringement rights are indeed exhausted.

Only if there is a real risk that national markets will be partitioned if the importer bears the burden of proof (particularly if the proprietor uses an exclusive distribution system in the EEA and could obstruct further purchases by the importer from a member of that exclusive distribution system if they were identified) will the burden of proof shift to the trade mark proprietor.

PEAK PERFORMANCE

Peak Holding AB v Axolin-Elinor AB
C-16/03, 30 November 2004

Contractual restrictions preventing the resale of goods cannot prevent goods from being deemed to be 'put on the market' where a sale has in fact taken place within the EEA. The proprietor's rights will therefore be exhausted once the goods are sold on.

Keywords
Exhaustion of rights & parallel imports; Article 7(1) TMD.

Issue
Peak Holding granted a licence to Peak Performance Production to use the mark PEAK PERFORMANCE in Sweden. Peak Performance subsequently sold surplus clothing items bearing the PEAK PERFORMANCE trade mark to a French company, but the sales agreement stated that the company could not resell the clothing items in Europe other than to Russia and Slovenia.

Items bearing the PEAK PERFORMANCE trade mark ended up in a third party retail outlet in Sweden. Peak Holding sued for trade mark infringement and the defendant claimed that Peak Holding had exhausted its rights due to either:

- importing the goods into the EEA;
- being offered for sale in shops (despite remaining unsold); or
- selling the items to the French company.

Ruling
The CJ held that the sale of goods to a party within the EEA constitutes goods being 'put on the market' in the EEA in accordance with Article 7(1) TMD regardless of the existence of a contractual prohibition on reselling in the EEA. However, where goods are simply imported into the EEA or offered for sale in the EEA but no sales are actually achieved, the proprietor's rights are not exhausted because the proprietor has not disposed of the goods to third parties and has not yet realised the economic value of the trade mark.

AQUAFRESH

Class International BV v Colgate-Palmolive Company,
Unilever NV, SmithKline Beecham Plc, Beecham Group Plc
C-405/03, 18 October 2005

**A trade mark owner cannot oppose the mere entry into
the Community of 'non-exhausted' goods, the goods
must actually be put on the market in the Community,
or the offer of their sale must necessarily lead to that
conclusion before a proprietor may object. Once customs
has been cleared, the goods are 'put on the market'.**

Keywords
Exhaustion of rights & parallel imports; goods in transit; Article 5(1) TMD;
Article 3(b) & (c) TMD; Article 9(1) CTMR; Article 2(b) & (c) CTMR.

Issue
Class International brought AQUAFRESH branded toothpaste from outside
the Community (South Africa) into the Community (Rotterdam). The goods
were seized by Beecham while they were still stored in transit. They had not
yet been put on the market in the Community. Questions referred to the CJ
included:

O Is the mere entry or warehousing of goods in the EC considered
   use in the course of trade which can be opposed by the proprietor?
O Can the proprietor object to such goods being marketed?
O Who bears the burden of proof in such circumstances?

Ruling
Provided that parallel imported goods are only in transit and no final
destination within the Community has been established, there can be no
trade mark infringement. To infringe, the relevant goods must be put on
the market in the Community as in PEAK PERFORMANCE (page 136).
If the offer of sale would necessarily involve the putting
of those goods on the market in the Community,
the trade mark owner may object. In such a
situation it is for the proprietor to prove
the facts of either free release into the
Community or an offering or sale of
the goods which necessarily entails
their being put on the market in
the Community.

COPAD v DIOR

Copad SA v Christian Dior Couture SA & Others
C-59/08, 23 April 2009

This guidance considerably strengthens the hand of
luxury brand owners to maintain and enforce a selective
distribution network for their products. Luxury brand
owners can now extend protection to the brand image
even if it is not an explicit term of a licence. Sellers further
down the supply chain will need to be more cautious
when selling goods bearing a 'luxury' trade mark.

Keywords

Exhaustion of rights & parallel imports; licences; resale; luxury brands; quality
control; Article 7 TMD; Article 8(2) TMD.

Issue

Dior sought to restrain Copad (a discount store) in the resale of Dior products
supplied to licensees and then sold to Copad. Dior argued this was in
contravention of the 'prestige' clauses of their licence and claimed that resale
in this way would damage the reputation and allure of Dior as a luxury brand.

Ruling

The CJ confirmed that a trade mark proprietor can invoke the rights conferred
by a registration against a licensee who contravenes a provision in a licence
agreement prohibiting, on the grounds of the trade mark's prestige, sales of
goods to discount stores. The proprietor needs to establish that the contravention
damages the allure and prestigious image which bestows on those goods an
'aura of luxury'.

A licensee who puts goods bearing a trade mark on the market in disregard of
a licence of this nature does so without the consent of the proprietor (ie, there
is no exhaustion of rights).

Where a licensee puts luxury goods on the market in contravention of a
provision in a licence agreement, the proprietor can rely on the licence to
oppose the resale of those goods if it can be established that such resale
damages the reputation of the trade mark.

TESTER BOTTLES OF PERFUME

Coty Prestige Lancaster Group GmbH v Simex Trading AG
C-127/09, 03 June 2010

'Tester' or 'demonstration' bottles of perfume can be prevented from sale within the EEA, even if they have been first supplied within the EEA, where there is no express or implied consent to them being placed on the market by the proprietor.

Keywords
Exhaustion of rights & parallel imports; Infringement; testers labelled "not for sale".

Issue
Coty detected testers of its perfumes for sale in a German supermarket. Such testers were supplied by Coty to selected distributors worldwide on terms that ownership remained with Coty and the products were not to be sold but only offered to consumers to test the perfume. The actual bottles were also labelled "tester" and "not for sale". Coty sought a prohibitory injunction against the supermarket's supplier. Simex opposed that application on the basis that Coty's rights had been exhausted because the testers had already been put on the market in the EEA with its consent.

At first instance, the action was dismissed on the basis that Coty's rights had been exhausted. On appeal, questions concerning whether the testers in issue had been put on the market were referred to the CJ.

Although the testers in issue seemed to have been first supplied outside the EEA, the case proceeded more generally on the issues of whether Coty could stop such sales (no matter where the products were first supplied).

Ruling
The CJ confirmed that the sale of the testers was carried out not by the proprietor or by its distributors but by Simex. The CJ ruled that the determining factor was whether there was express or implied consent by Coty. It was necessary to look at the goods in issue and the intention of Coty. The fact that legal ownership remained with Coty and that the products were labelled "demonstration" and "not for sale" were decisive factors precluding a finding that Coty expressly or implicitly consented to the goods being put on the market. The statements in particular reflect the intention of Coty that the goods bearing its mark should not be sold to consumers in or outside of the EEA.

GAS BOTTLES
Viking Gas A/S v Kosan Gas A/S
C-46/10, 14 July 2011

A proprietor of a mark may not prevent use of its mark
where it has realised economic value attached to that
mark (ie, through sales) and where the further
commercialisation by a third party is not carried out in
such a way as to suggest a false commercial connection
between the proprietor and the third party.

Keywords
Exhaustion of rights & parallel imports; legitimate reasons for opposing further
commercialisation; re-usable packaging.

Issue
Kosan Gas produced and sold bottled gas. The bottle shape was registered
as a 3D CTM (for gaseous fuels and containers used for liquid fuels), as were
Kosan's name and logo, which were also affixed to the bottles. Kosan's
customers paid for the bottle as well as the gas, and the bottles were
designed to be refilled. Viking sold gas in Kosan's composite gas bottles.
Kosan sued Viking for trade mark infringement in Denmark and succeeded at
first instance because it was held that Viking was infringing Kosan's rights by
filling and marketing composite bottles. On appeal, the Danish Supreme
Court referred a number of questions to the CJ.

Ruling
The CJ held that the bottles did not constitute mere packaging; they had an
independent economic value and must be regarded as goods in themselves.
Kosan's sale of the bottles enabled it to realise the economic value of the marks
relating to those bottles.

Further, the purchaser could not fully enjoy its property rights in the bottles if
those rights were restricted by the related trade mark rights belonging to Kosan.
To allow Kosan to prevent the bottles from being refilled by third parties would
unduly reduce competition on the downstream market for refilling bottles.
Accordingly, Kosan's exclusive rights were exhausted.

Finally, Viking's treatment of the bottles (adding its own name alongside
Kosan's) did not entitle Kosan to oppose that commercialisation, unless it was
not carried out in such a way as to give a false impression to the average
consumer that there was a commercial connection between Viking and Kosan.

ORIFARM

Orifarm A/S & Others and Paranova Denmark A/S & Others
v Merck Sharp & Dohme Corp & Others
Joined cases C-400/09 & C-207/10, 28 July 2011

It is acceptable for a repackaged product not to indicate
the actual re-packager, if the consumer is not misled into
believing that the trade mark proprietor is responsible for
the repackaging.

Keywords
Exhaustion of rights & parallel imports; repackaging; Article 7 CTMR.

Issue
In both cases, Merck brought the action on the basis that the name of the
actual re-packager of the products did not appear on the repackaging. The
names of the holders of the authorisation to market and sell the products were
on the packaging, rather than the names of the companies that carried out the
repackaging, which were holders of authorisations to do so. Merck was
initially successful in both cases. On appeal, the relevant Danish court
referred questions to the CJ to establish whether Article 7(2) CTMR should be
interpreted as meaning that a proprietor of a mark can oppose the further
marketing of repackaged pharmaceutical products when the new packaging
"indicates as the repackager not the undertaking which, on instructions,
actually repackaged the product and holds an authorisation to do so, but the
undertaking which holds the marketing authorisation for the product, on
whose instructions the repackaging was carried out, and which assumes
liability for the repackaging".

Ruling
The CJ ruled that Article 7(2) CTMR does not allow the proprietor of a mark to
oppose the further marketing on the above grounds because the consumer is
not misled into thinking that the proprietor is responsible for the packaging.
Further, the proprietor can still take action should the condition of the product
have been affected by the repackaging because the undertaking identified on
the packaging as the re-packager will remain liable for any damage. If the
repackaging is carried out in conditions which cannot affect the original
condition of the product inside the packaging, the essential function of the
trade mark as a guarantee of origin is safeguarded.

D YOUNG&CO
REVOCATION&
GENUINE USE

MINIMAX

Ansul BV v Ajax Brandbeveiliging BV
C-40/01, 11 March 2003

The term 'genuine use' extends beyond sales of new products on the market but also includes maintaining and supplying parts for such goods under which the mark was originally marketed.

Keywords
Revocation & genuine use; Article 12(1) TMD.

Issue
Ansul was the proprietor of the trade mark MINIMAX for various goods including fire extinguishers and associated products. Ansul had not used the trade mark on new products for over five years but had maintained, checked and repaired existing equipment. Their registrations were challenged by Ajax on the grounds of non-use. The question of what constitutes genuine use was referred to the CJ.

Ruling
The CJ held that genuine use is where the trade mark is used in accordance with its essential function, ie, to guarantee the identity of the origin of the goods/services for which it is registered. This use must not be merely token use, serving only to preserve the rights conferred by the mark, or of a nature which is purely internal use by the proprietor. With regard to what constitutes genuine use, the CJ confirmed this must be assessed taking into account the nature of the goods/services at issue, the characteristics of the market and scale and frequency of use. This means that in certain markets, use need not always be quantitatively significant for it to be deemed genuine. Importantly, genuine use of a trade mark must be to create or maintain a share of the market of the goods/services covered by the mark.

The CJ concluded by confirming that use of a trade mark may, in certain circumstances, be held as genuine where the goods are no longer available for purchase, ie, in the provision of an after-sales service such as the sale of accessories or related parts, or in the supply of maintenance and repair services.

The CJ then referred the case back to the Benelux courts, whereby, based on this clarification from the CJ, they found that Ansul's provision of such after-sales activities did amount to genuine use of MINIMAX and therefore the revocation actions were rejected.

LA MER

La Mer Technology Inc v Laboratoires Goemar SA
C-259/02, 27 January 2004

Genuine use of a mark after the filing of the revocation
action is not necessarily irrelevant and the court should,
in some circumstances, take this into account.

Keywords
Revocation & genuine use; evidence after filing revocation action; Article
10(1) TMD; Article 12(1) TMD.

Issue
La Mer applied to revoke Goemar's registration for LABORATOIRE DE LA
MER claiming non-use in the preceding five year period. The EWHC asked
the CJ what factors should be taken into account when deciding whether a
mark has been put to genuine use.

Specifically, the EWHC asked (amongst other questions already answered
in MINIMAX (page 146) whether it was necessary to disregard use occurring
after the filing of the application for revocation, even for the purpose of
deciding whether use during the relevant period was genuine.

Ruling
The CJ reaffirmed the position as previously set out in Ansul. In particular
it said that minimal and quantitatively insignificant use may be genuine,
provided it is justified in the sector concerned for the purpose of creating
or preserving a market share for the goods concerned.

The CJ also indicated that a relatively low volume of goods marketed under the
trade mark may be compensated by high intensity/value. For example, use by
a single company importing goods may be sufficient if the import operation
has a genuine commercial justification.

In answer to the EWHC's question regarding use made after the filing of the
revocation, the CJ said that the TMD does not preclude, in assessing the
genuineness of use during the relevant period, account being taken, where
appropriate, of these circumstances.

ELIZABETH EMANUEL

Elizabeth Florence Emanuel v Continental Shelf 128 Ltd
C-259/04, 30 March 2006

This case highlights the careful consideration required
when assigning personal trade marks, as once the mark
has been assigned, the applicant may lose control over their
name and may not be able to trade under it in the future.

Keywords

Revocation & genuine use; assignments; personal names; goodwill; Article
3(1)(g) TMD; Article 12(2)(b) TMD.

Issue

Clothing designer Elizabeth Emanuel assigned a trade mark consisting of
her name together with the associated goodwill. The registration was then
assigned once more to Continental. Elizabeth Emanuel subsequently sought
to revoke the mark on the basis that it was deceptive to the public, which
might believe she was still involved with the design or creation of the goods.
The CJ was asked for a preliminary ruling on the issue.

Ruling

The CJ stated that a trade mark corresponding to the name of the designer
and first manufacturer of the goods (in this case ELIZABETH EMANUEL)
bearing that mark may not be refused registration on the grounds that it would
deceive the public, within the meaning of Article 3(1)(g) TMD, in particular
where the goodwill associated with that trade mark has been assigned
together with the business. Further, a trade mark corresponding to the name
of the designer and first manufacturer of goods bearing that trade mark, is also
not liable to revocation on the grounds that that mark would mislead the
public within the meaning of Article 12(2)(b) TMD; in such circumstances.
Elizabeth Emanuel was not, therefore, successful.

VITAFRUIT

The Sunrider Corp v OHIM (Mr Espadafor Caba)
C-416/04, 11 May 2006

This case is of particular significance as it reiterates that acceptable proof of genuine use is not dependent on sales volumes and there is no *de minimis* rule.

Keywords

Revocation & genuine use; proof of use; token use; Article 8(1)(b) CTMR; Article 15(3) CTMR; Article 43(2) CTMR; Article (3) CTMR.

Issue

Sunrider argued that the level of use demonstrated by Mr Caba was not sufficient to constitute genuine use as required by Article 43(2) CTMR. They argued that in view of the fact that the goods protected by the earlier mark were intended for daily use by consumers and, as they were quite cheap, the goods should be easy to sell in quantity. Therefore, the sales figures provided were very low. The invoices indicated that all sales had been to one party and only consisted of five transactions over a period of eleven months. The suggestion was that the sales were only token and made to keep the mark valid, rather than showing a genuine trade in the goods.

Ruling

Whilst agreeing that all factors, such as level of use, should be taken into account when assessing whether such use was genuine, the CJ upheld the GC's view that genuine use is that which identifies the origin of a product and is intended to create or preserve an outlet for the goods. Genuine use does not include token use intended solely to preserve rights in a trade mark. All the facts and circumstances in each case must be considered in order to decide whether token or true commercial use has taken place.

The CJ agreed that the sales in this case had been relatively low for the type of products; nevertheless, there is no *de minimis* rule. So long as the use serves a real commercial purpose, even a relatively small amount of use can be sufficient to establish genuine use. The CJ reaffirmed that sales in a limited geographical area of one EU member state could also be considered sufficient and genuine use.

HÄUPL v LIDL

Armin Häupl v Lidl Stiftung & Co KG
C-246/05, 14 June 2007

Unhelpfully, the CJ stated that the "date of completion of the registration procedure" should be determined under national laws. The assessment on whether there are genuine reasons why the trade mark has not been used will be determined on a case-by-case basis, these must generally be outside the control of the proprietor.

Keywords
Revocation & genuine use; date of completion of registration procedure; Article 10(1) TMD; Article 12(1) TMD.

Issue
Lidl owned the mark LE CHEF DE CUISINE in various countries including an IR designating Austria. Mr Häupl sought cancellation of the trade mark in Austria on the grounds of non-use. In his view, the five year period for the cancellation action began from the protection period, namely 12 October 1993. Lidl challenged the application for cancellation and submitted that the five year non-use period began later.

Two questions were referred to the CJ. The first question regarded the meaning of the 'date of completion of the registration procedure'. The second question was "are there proper grounds for non-use of a trade mark if the implementation of the corporate strategy pursued by the proprietor of the trade mark is delayed for reasons outside its control, or is the trade mark proprietor obliged to change his corporate strategy in order to use the trade mark in good time?".

Ruling
Regarding the date of completion of the registration procedure, the CJ said that its meaning must be determined in each member state in accordance with the procedural rules in force in that state. On the second question the CJ held that only obstacles having sufficient direct relationship with the trade mark, making its use impossible or unreasonable, and which arise independently of the will of the proprietor of that mark, may be described as proper reasons for non-use of that mark. It is the task of the national court or tribunal, before which the dispute in the main proceedings is brought to establish the relevant facts, and apply that assessment in the context of the present action.

WELLNESS

Silberquelle GmbH v Maselli-Strickmode GmbH
C-495/07, 15 January 2009

In order to support genuine use, actual sales of goods or services are required. Mere promotional use does not amount to genuine use.

Keywords
Revocation & genuine use; promotional use; Article 10 TMD; Article 12 TMD.

Issue
Maselli manufactures and sells clothes. It owned a registration for the mark WELLNESS covering classes 16, 25 and 32. Class 32 covers alcohol-free drinks. Whilst selling clothing, Maselli used the trade mark WELLNESS to designate an alcohol-free drink which was handed out as a gift in bottles marked "WELLNESS-DRINK" along with the clothing sold. In its promotional documents, Maselli made reference to the free gifts labelled with the WELLNESS mark. Maselli did not use the mark for drinks sold separately. Silberquelle, which sells alcohol-free drinks, applied to have the trade mark cancelled. The question referred to the CJ was whether a trade mark was put to genuine use if it was used for goods which the proprietor gave free of charge to purchasers of his other goods, after the conclusion of the transaction.

Ruling
The CJ held that the condition of genuine use is not fulfilled where promotional items are handed out as a reward for the purchase of other goods and to encourage the sale of the latter. Those items are not distributed in any way with the owner penetrating the market for goods in the same class. In those circumstances, affixing the mark to those items does not contribute to creating an outlet for those items or to distinguishing, in the interests of the customer, those items from the goods of other undertakings. Further, the CJ stated that "genuine use must be interpreted as meaning that where a proprietor of a mark affixes that mark to items that it gives, free of charge, to purchasers of its goods, it does not make genuine use of that mark in respect of the class covering those items".

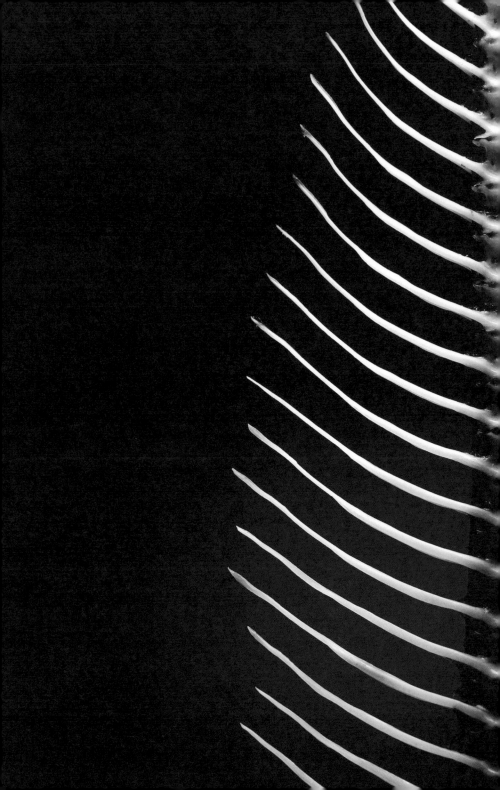

FISHBONE BEACHWEAR

New Yorker SHK Jeans GmbH & Co KG v OHIM
C-621/11, 18 July 2011

Additional evidence may be considered where new factors emerge and the evidence is relevant, even if that evidence is adduced after the expiry of the period set by the Opposition Division. An accumulation of items of evidence, which taken individually, would be insufficient, allows necessary facts to be established and have probative value insofar as they corroborate other elements in the file. Where a mark contains a descriptive element in the registration and the evidence does not include the descriptive term, this evidence may still be taken into account for the purposes of showing proof of use.

Keywords

Revocation & genuine use; additional evidence; non-use of descriptive elements; Article 42 CTMR; Article 76(2) CTMR.

Issue

A CTM application for FISHBONE in classes 18 and 25 was opposed by New Yorker SHK Jeams GmbH (SHK) under Article 8(1)(b) CTMR and Article 8(4) CTMR, based on an earlier Greek figurative registration for FISHBONE BEACHWEAR in class 25 (see right). SHK was required to furnish 'proof of use' of its mark. In the applicant's view, the evidence was insufficient to prove genuine use. The Opposition Division accepted further evidence and upheld the opposition for all goods in class 25 and "bags and rucksacks" in class 18. The applicant appealed. The Board of Appeal allowed the appeal in part. It said the Opposition Division was right to consider the additional evidence, that there was sufficient genuine use overall and there was a likelihood of confusion in respect of class 25.

Ruling

The CJ upheld the GC's decision and rejected the plea that the additional evidence should have been disregarded by the Board of Appeal; additional evidence may be considered where new factors emerge and where the evidence is relevant, even if it is submitted out of time. The GC confirmed that the evidence was sufficient to prove genuine use. The items of evidence, taken individually, may not be sufficient but accumulatively, they may have probative value and corroborate other elements. Where a mark contains a descriptive element and the evidence does not include the descriptive term (BEACHWEAR here), this evidence may still be taken into account for the purposes of showing proof of use.

ONEL/OMEL

Leno Merken BV v Hagelkruis Beheer BV
C-149/11, 19 December 2012

Use of a CTM in a single member state of the EU may not
be enough to constitute genuine use.

Keywords
Revocation & genuine use; Article 15(1) CTMR.

Issue
The question before the CJ in this case was whether use of a CTM in a single
member state of the EU constituted genuine use for the purposes of Article
15(1) CTMR, ie, when a CTM is vulnerable to revocation on the grounds of
lack of genuine use. Prior to this ruling, parties could rely on a joint statement
and opposition guidelines issued by the EU Commission/Council and OHIM
respectively that suggested use in one member state was enough to establish
genuine use throughout the EU.

Ruling
Article 15(1) CTMR must be interpreted as meaning that the territorial borders
of the member states should be disregarded in the assessment of whether a
trade mark has been put to 'genuine use in the Community' within the
meaning of that provision. It is for national courts to assess whether
conditions are met, taking into account all relevant facts and circumstances,
including the characteristics of the market concerned, the nature of the
goods/services protected by the trade mark and the territorial extent and the
scale of the use as well as its frequency and regularity.

A CTM is put to genuine use when it is used in accordance with its essential
function and for the purpose of maintaining or creating market share within
the European Community for the goods/services covered by it. Use in one
member state may not be enough to constitute genuine use of a mark.

The CJ refused to state a *de minimis* rule as to how much territorial use will
satisfy the requirements. The lack of such a benchmark will make it difficult to
predict how national courts will apply this ruling going forward.

LEVI'S

Colloseum Holding AG v Levi Strauss & Co
C-12/12, 18 April 2013

Genuine use of a trade mark (which has become distinctive through use as one of the elements of another composite mark) is possible, even if only used in conjunction with another registered mark and even if the combination of the two marks is also registered.

Keywords

Revocation & genuine use; composite marks; device marks; distinctiveness; Article 15(1) CTMR.

Issue

Levi owned the mark LEVI'S; a device mark of a back pocket with a blank red tag (below left); and a similar device with a red tag containing the word LEVI'S (below right). Colloseum made jeans with a red tag on the back pocket, on which appeared names of various brands. Levi sued in Germany for trade mark infringement. Colloseum claimed non-use in relation to the blank tag device mark (below right).

The CJ was asked whether there was genuine use of the second mark where it had gained distinctiveness only through use of the first mark; or where it was used only in conjunction with the word mark, the public considered the two marks to be independent distinctive signs and the combination of the two marks was itself a registered trade mark.

Ruling

There can be genuine use of a registered mark (such as above left) where it is used only within a composite mark or in conjunction with another mark even when the composite mark is itself registered. Nevertheless, a mark that is used only as part of a composite mark or in conjunction with another mark must continue to be perceived as an indicator of origin in its own right for such use to count as genuine.

SPECSAVERS

Specsavers International Healthcare Ltd & Others v Asda Stores Ltd
C-252/12, 18 July 2013

Genuine use of a wordless logo may be shown by use of the logo with superimposed words; the colour in which a mark is used (and the context of use) may be decisive in assessing infringement.

Keywords
Revocation & genuine use; likelihood of confusion; reputation; Article 15(1) CTMR; Article 9(1)(b) & (c) CTMR.

Issue
Specsavers owned three logo registrations, each comprising two overlapping ovals. Two of the marks had the word SPECSAVERS written across the ovals; the third did not. Could use of the first two marks constitute genuine use of the third? The marks had historically been used in a dark green. When considering infringement, to what extent was this relevant? Was it relevant what colour Asda's marks were, or that Asda was itself associated with the colour green?

Ruling
The CJ held that use of the wordless logo with the word SPECSAVERS superimposed on top may be considered use of the wordless logo to the extent that the wordless logo always refers in that form to the goods covered by the registration (a matter for the referring court to assess). It did not matter that the word mark and the combined word/logo were also registered. The CTMR allowed variations of marks (that do not alter their distinctive character) to constitute genuine use, thereby enabling owners to adapt marketing techniques without fear of their marks being vulnerable to attack for non-use.

The CJ confirmed that the likelihood of confusion/unfair advantage must be assessed globally. How the marks are perceived by consumers plays a decisive role. The colour in which a mark is used affects consumer perception and therefore may increase the likelihood of confusion, and any unfair advantage taken.

Assessments of infringement must take account of the context in which an allegedly infringing sign is used (see O2 v HUTCHISON 3G, page 116). The fact that Asda was itself associated with the colour green may be important: this could result in a lower likelihood of confusion because consumers may perceive it as Asda's colour – a matter for the English court to determine. Asda's association with the colour green could also be relevant in determining whether there was 'due cause' when assessing unfair advantage/detriment.

D YOUNG&CO
INVALIDITY

BOSTONGURKA

Björnekulla Fruktindustrier AB v Procordia Food AB
C-371/02, 29 April 2004

The UK has historically placed an emphasis on the perception of the relevant trade when assessing whether a mark has become generic. This ruling makes it clear that the views of consumers and/or users and also intermediaries (where applicable) are also relevant in revocation actions.

Keywords
Invalidity; revocation; generic trade marks; relevant class of persons; Article 12(2)(a) TMD.

Issue
Björnekulla sought to revoke the trade mark BOSTONGURKA in Sweden on the grounds that the mark had become a generic term for chopped pickled gherkins as a result of the acts or inactivity of Procordia.

Ruling
The CJ held that, when assessing the question of whether a mark has become generic under Article 12(2)(a) TMD, the perception of consumers and users will play a decisive role. Furthermore, the CJ held that where intermediaries are involved in the distribution of the products, their views may also be taken into account in assessing whether the mark has become generic for the goods in question.

The CJ said, "In general, the perception of consumers or end users will play a decisive role...Accordingly, the relevant classes of person comprise principally consumers and end users".

BSS

Alcon Inc v OHIM (Dr Robert Winzer Pharma GmbH)
C-192/03, 05 October 2004

Evidence that post dates the date of filing of the application may be taken into account in invalidation proceedings if it indicates what the position would have been like at the relevant date.

Keywords

Invalidity; registrability; generic terms; Article 7 CTMR.

Issue

The mark BSS was registered by Alcon for ophthalmic solutions. The intervener in the proceedings filed an action against the registration on the basis that it was invalid. It submitted that BSS was an abbreviation for 'balanced salt solution' or 'buffered saline solution'. Evidence showed that pharmaceutical articles and dictionaries described BSS as a generic term which was also in use by third parties.

Ruling

The CJ held that it was not simply the fact that the mark was being used descriptively that was decisive but that the current usage was in the relevant sector.

Also, in invalidity proceedings, the CJ held that the relevant date at which the conflict must be examined is the date of filing of the challenged mark, although documents from a later date may be relevant and taken into account if they shed some light on the position at the relevant date.

LINDT

Chocoladefabriken Lindt & Sprüngli AG v Franz Hauswirth GmbH
C-529/07, 11 June 2009

The list of considerations in this case is not exhaustive but indicates that emphasis will be placed on the applicant's motivation where bad faith is concerned. Each case is to be decided on its own facts, however, this case may prove to be an important precedent.

Keywords
Invalidity; bad faith; 3D trade marks; Article 51(1)(b) CTMR.

Issue
Lindt and Hauswirth had produced similar chocolate Easter bunnies for over 50 years. Lindt registered a 3D mark of a foil wrapped chocolate bunny as a CTM and then brought infringement proceedings against Hauswirth, who counter-claimed for invalidity of Lindt's CTM on the basis of bad faith under Article 52(1)(b) CTMR. The referring Austrian court found there was a likelihood of confusion, but asked the CJ for guidance on the criteria to apply when determining whether Lindt had acted in bad faith.

The CJ was asked whether an applicant would be acting in bad faith if its application was filed with a view to preventing a competitor from continuing to use a sign which could be confused with the mark for similar goods/services.

Ruling
The CJ said the national court has to consider whether, at the time of filing the application for registration:

○ the applicant knew or must have known that the third party was using, in at least one member state, an identical or similar sign for an identical or similar product capable of being confused with the sign for which registration was sought;

○ the applicant intended to prevent that third party from continuing to use such a sign;

○ the respective signs enjoyed any degree of legal protection.

COLOR EDITION

Lancôme parfums et beauté & Cie SNC v OHIM (CMS Hasche Sigle)
C-408/08, 25 February 2010

Acceptance and registration of a trade mark by OHIM does not necessarily mean the sign is distinctive.

Keywords
Invalidity; registrability; Article 55(1)(a) CTMR; Article 7(1)(c) CTMR.

Issue
A law firm applied to invalidate the registration of the trade mark COLOR EDITION for cosmetic and make-up preparations on the grounds that the trade mark was descriptive and devoid of distinctive character. The CJ was asked to rule first on whether a law firm could bring such an action and second on the registrability of COLOR EDITION.

Ruling
The CJ said that an action under Article 55(1)(a) CTMR based on an absolute ground for invalidity may be submitted by any natural or legal person and any group or body set up for the purpose of representing the interests of manufacturers, producers, suppliers of services, traders or consumers, which have the capacity in their own name to sue and be sued. However, no decisive ruling was given in this case because this issue had not been raised before the GC and was outside the remit of the appeal.

The CJ agreed with the ruling of the GC in connection with the registrability of the mark COLOR EDITION in that the combination of 'color' and 'edition' was not unusual but a normal construction in light of the lexical rules of the English language, and that the mark did not create an impression sufficiently removed from that produced by the simple juxtaposition of the verbal elements of which it was composed to alter its meaning or scope. The mark was descriptive.

LEGO

Lego Juris A/S v OHIM (Mega Brands Inc)
C-48/09, 14 September 2010

The decision of the CJ that technical solutions cannot be subject to monopoly trade mark rights is a blow for Lego, whose trade mark was found, in fact, to be distinctive for the goods. Although this was outside the scope of the current proceedings, the CJ did acknowledge that the matter could be considered in light of unfair competition; however currently the EU has no provisions for this.

Keywords
Invalidity; shapes & 3D marks; shapes necessary to obtain a technical result; Article 7(1)(e)(ii) CTMR.

Issue
Mega Brands applied to OHIM to invalidate Lego's 3D trade mark for the distinctive red brick shape.

Following invalidation of the trade mark by OHIM, Lego appealed all the way up to the CJ for a finding that its trade mark was not invalid.

Ruling
The CJ held that the brick shape was invalid because its shape was necessary to obtain a technical result. The fact that the shape of the bricks could take many forms did not preclude its technical function. The CJ also held that the assessment of technical functionality of the mark applied for may take into account patent documents describing the functional elements of the shape concerned.

The question of distinctiveness acquired through use has no bearing on the refusal of a mark on the grounds of a shape necessary to obtain a technical result, hence Lego's trade mark was considered to be outside the scope of registrability under the CTMR.

YAKULT BOTTLE

Malaysia Dairy Industries Pte Ltd v Ankenævnet for Patenter og Varemærker
C-320/12, 27 June 2013

Assessment of the concept of bad faith.

Keywords
Invalidity; bad faith; Article 4(4)(g) TMD.

Issue
Malaysia Dairy applied for a 3D trade mark in Denmark in the shape of a bottle. Yakult opposed the application claiming that Malaysia Dairy had acted in bad faith, as it knew, or should have known, that Yakult held a number of rights in other countries for its own similar bottle shape.

Prior to this decision, it was sufficient to demonstrate evidence that there was prior, actual or presumed knowledge of the earlier trade marks in order to establish bad faith, and therefore to object to a later-filed application.

Ruling
The CJ held that the fact that a party is aware of a confusingly similar trade mark in other countries when applying for a mark cannot be held to be conclusive evidence of bad faith in and by itself. This factor must be taken into account as part of a global assessment of all relevant factors on a case-by-case basis. The CJ highlighted that in particular, the applicant's intention must be considered, which, being a subjective matter, must be determined by reference to the objective circumstances of the particular case.

The CJ emphasised that bad faith, within the meaning of Article 4(4)(g) TMD, is an "autonomous concept of EU law", which should be applied consistently across the EU, and in particular, in the same manner as in the context of Article 52(1)(b) CTMR.

D YOUNG&CO
CTM PROCEDURE &
PRACTICE

POSTKANTOOR

Koninklijke KPN Nederland NV v Benelux-Merkenbureau
C-363/99, 12 February 2004

This decision is an example of the CJ's retreat from BABY-DRY, raising the bar for acceptance of composite trade marks which consist of potentially descriptive elements. To be registrable, the combination produced must be more than the mere sum of its parts. This case also led to a significant change of practice regarding exclusions from the specification.

Keywords

CTM procedure & practice; absolute grounds; distinctive character; descriptiveness; disclaimers; Article 3(1) TMD.

Issue

The Dutch Post Office filed an application in the Benelux for the mark POSTKANTOOR (meaning 'post office') for a diverse range of goods and services including postage stamps, insurance and telecommunications. Following a reference from the Dutch court, the CJ considered the registrability criteria under Article 3 TMD (corresponding to Article 7(1)(b) & (c) CTMR).

Ruling

The CJ held that where registration of a mark is sought in respect of various goods/services, the competent authority must check, in relation to each of the goods/services claimed, that none of the grounds for refusal apply. The authority may reach different conclusions in respect of each of the goods/services. A combination of descriptive elements brought together without introducing any unusual variations, in particular as to syntax or meaning, cannot result in a registrable trade mark. The combination must create an impression which is sufficiently far removed from that produced by the simple combination of those elements.

The fact that the same mark may have been registered by another member state is irrelevant and negative disclaimers cannot assist. The TMD prevents registration of a trade mark for certain goods/services "on condition that they do not possess" a particular characteristic. It was previously the UKIPO's practice to allow exclusions in respect of marks which were descriptive of goods in the specification having certain characteristics, but acceptable for the same goods without that characteristic. This is no longer possible.

GLAVERBEL

Glaverbel SA v OHIM
C-445/02, 28 June 2004

Whilst the decision on the inherent registrability of this mark is perhaps not surprising given the current trend of European case law, it is another reminder of the CJ's remit to only hear appeals on points of law.

Keywords
CTM procedure & practice; absolute grounds; appeals on points of law; Article 7(1)(b) CTMR.

Issue
Glaverbel applied for a CTM with the description that the mark comprised a design applied to the surface of the goods, in respect of glass products, sanitary fittings and installations. The GC had held that the design, as applied to the surface of the glass sheet, formed part of the decorative appearance of the product itself and would also be perceived as the technical means by which the glass was rendered opaque. The GC stated that it would not be viewed as an indication of trade origin.

Ruling
The CJ agreed with the GC and dismissed the appeal.

Appellate tribunals may only consider the contested decision made by the lower tribunal and, once before the CJ, the court may only consider points of law; they cannot re-examine findings of fact made by the GC and lower tribunals unless the clear sense of the evidence produced earlier is distorted. Arguments relating to the distortion of the sense of the evidence must be included to be considered.

PRAKTIKER

Praktiker Bau und Heimwerkermärkte AG
v Deutsches Patent und Markekamt
C-418/02, 07 July 2005

To properly claim 'retail services' it is necessary to list
the goods or the type of goods for which protection for
the services is sought, ie, 'retail services connected with
the sale of [list goods]'.

Keywords

CTM procedure & practice; absolute grounds; registrability of services in the
retail trade; Article 2 TMD; Article 4(1)(b) TMD; Article 5(1)(b) TMD.

Issue

Praktiker applied to register the trade mark PRAKTIKER in relation to retail
trade in building, home improvement, gardening and other consumer goods
for the do-it-yourself (DIY) sector. The application was rejected because
it was considered that the concept 'retail trade' did not denote independent
services. The economic activities which formed the core of goods
distribution, in particular the purchase and sale of goods, were not services
for which a trade mark could be registered. Trade mark protection could be
achieved only by applying for registration of the trade mark in connection
with the goods distributed in each case.

However, Praktiker argued that "... the economic trend towards a service
society necessitated a re-appraisal of the retail trade as a service ..." and that
consumers would "... increasingly be influenced not only by the availability
and price of a product, but also by other aspects such as the variety and
assortment of goods, their presentation, the service provided by staff,
advertising, image and the location of the store, etc. Such services provided
in connection with retail trade enabled retailers to be distinguishable from their
competitors and ought to be eligible for protection by service trade marks."
The point was referred to the CJ.

Ruling

The CJ held that the concept of 'services' covers services provided in
connection with retail trade in goods. For the purposes of registration of
the trade mark for such services, it is not necessary to specify in detail the
services in question. However, details must be provided in connection with
the goods or type of goods to which those services relate.

SISSI ROSSI

Sergio Rossi SpA v OHIM (Sissi Rossi Srl)
C-214/05, 18 July 2006

The decision reiterates that the powers of the appellate courts are to review errors of law, and in the absence of any errors, the courts should not overturn the decisions of the lower authorities. Appeals are not to be used as a forum for presenting new evidence and arguments, although in some circumstances new evidence may be submitted before the Board of Appeal (see ARCOL, page 176).

Keywords
CTM procedure & practice; late evidence; additional arguments on appeal; Article 8(1)(b) CTMR.

Issue
Sissi Rossi's CTM application for SISSI ROSSI covering goods in class 18 was opposed by Sergio Rossi on the basis of Italian and French registrations for MISS ROSSI covering 'footwear' in class 25.

The Board of Appeal overturned the decision to uphold the opposition, finding that there was only vague similarity between the marks and that the differences between the goods (footwear and bags) outweighed any similarities. The GC refused to take evidence presented for the first time into account and held that there was no likelihood of confusion. Sergio Rossi appealed to the CJ.

Ruling
Efforts to include relevant facts and evidence for the first time before the GC could not be accepted. The CJ confirmed that the role of the Community courts is confined to a legal review of the legality of the decision and is not a re-examination of the facts which were assessed by OHIM. OHIM's assessment is limited to the facts which are put forward by the parties during the proceedings and its decisions cannot be challenged on the basis of facts not known to it at the time of the decision.

ARCOL
Kaul GmbH v OHIM (Bayer AG)
C-193/09, 04 March 2010

Evidence can, in certain circumstances, be submitted for the first time before the Board of Appeal. However, no broadening of arguments or filing of additional evidence will be accepted before either the GC or CJ (see SISSI ROSSI, page 174).

Keywords
CTM procedure & practice; late evidence; additional arguments on appeal; Article 74(2) CTMR.

Issue
Bayer's application for the CTM ARCOL was opposed by Kaul GmbH on the basis of their earlier rights in the trade mark CAPOL. The case turned on whether Kaul could file additional arguments on appeal, effectively broadening the scope of their opposition, and also submit new evidence despite the initial rejection by OHIM.

Ruling
The CJ held that there was no principle precluding the Board of Appeal from taking into account facts and evidence produced for the first time at the appeal stage. Indeed, an examination of the jurisdiction of the Board of Appeal supported the view that it was called upon to carry out a new, full examination of the merits of the case, both in terms of law and facts.

The CJ held that the Board of Appeal is entitled to disregard facts or evidence which are filed out of time; however, the Board of Appeal is not automatically prohibited from taking account of such facts and evidence even where they are submitted or produced late. Parties do not have an unconditional right to file facts and evidence out of time. Article 74(2) CTMR grants OHIM a wide discretion. Taking late filed evidence into account on appeal may be justified if it is relevant to the outcome.

WEBSHIPPING

DHL Express France SAS v Chronopost SA
C-235/09, 12 April 2011

The CJ confirmed that injunctions and 'coercive measures' granted by national courts in CTM infringement cases should have effect throughout the EU. However, where there is no infringement or threatened infringement in certain parts of the EU, it may still be possible to argue that there should be territorial limitations on the measures ordered by the court. In such cases the onus will be on the defendant to show why pan-EU relief should not be granted.

Keywords

CTM procedure & practice; territorial Scope; Article 1 CTMR; Article 98(1) CTMR; Brussels Regulation.

Issue

Chronopost is the proprietor of French and CTM registrations for the mark WEBSHIPPING. DHL was using signs including WEB SHIPPING in relation to identical services. Chronopost sued DHL before the designated Community Trade Mark Court in France for trade mark infringement of both registrations and succeeded before the Court of Appeal in Paris. Chronopost appealed further to the Court of Cassation due to the Court of Appeal's failure to explicitly state that the injunction restraining further infringement of the CTM extended to the whole of the EU. The Court of Cassation had doubts as to the interpretation of Article 98 and referred questions to the CJ for a preliminary ruling.

Ruling

The CJ ruled that an injunction issued by a Community court should, as a rule, have effect throughout the whole of the EU. However, it also stated that there could be certain circumstances in which the territorial scope of the injunction could be restricted. Further, where a court attaches 'coercive measures' to a prohibition by application of its national law (for example, the order of a periodic payment penalty in case the injunction were to be breached) these too are applicable within the territories of the member states in which that prohibition would have effect. If such coercive measures are not contained in the national law of a member state, the objective pursued by that measure must be attained by the competent court of that member state by having recourse to the relevant provisions of national law which are such as to ensure that the prohibition is complied with in an equivalent manner.

RIZO

Génesis Seguros Generales Sociedad Anónima de
Seguros y Reaseguros (Génesis) v Boys Toys SA
C-190/10, 22 March 2012

**The hour and minute of the filing of a CTM cannot be
taken into account when priority over a national trade
mark filed on the same day is being considered.**

Keywords
CTM procedure & practice; date and time of filing; Article 27 CTMR.

Issue
On 12 December 2003, Génesis filed two electronic applications at OHIM for
the marks 'Rizo' and 'Rizo, El Erizo', at 11.52 and 12.13 respectively. That
same day, Pool Angel Tomás SL applied to register Rizo's at the Spanish
Trade Marks Office at 17.45. Génesis opposed the Spanish application on the
basis that it enjoyed priority because its CTM applications were filed earlier
than the Spanish application. The Spanish Trade Marks Office refused the
opposition and Génesis appealed to the High Court in Madrid and then,
further, to the Tribunal Supremo who referred a question to the CJ. The
question sought clarification on Article 27 CTMR and whether that should be
interpreted as meaning the hour and minute of filing a CTM application should
be taken into account when priority is being considered over a national trade
mark application filed on the same day.

Ruling
The CJ examined the CTMR and found that it contains no express reference
to the hour and minute of filing and no reference to the hour or minute in the
communication issued by the office following receipt of a new application.
Furthermore, if an applicant chooses to file a CTM via its local Trade Mark
Office, there is no obligation to record the hour and minute of the filing.

The CJ concluded that the CTMR does not require the hour and minute of
filing to be taken into account in relation to a new CTM and that EU law
precludes the hour and minute of the filing of a CTM from being taken into
account for the purposes of establishing priority over a national trade mark
filed the same day. To do otherwise would undermine the uniform nature of
the protection of a CTM and could lead to a divergence as to the extent of
protection given to a CTM between member states.

OUTBURST

Paul Alfons Rehbein (GmbH & Co) KG v OHIM
T-214/08, 28 March 2012

The GC confirmed that the Board of Appeal does have discretion to accept new evidence provided that evidence merely complements, supplements, strengthens or clarifies the evidence submitted in time before the Opposition Division and there being no provision to the contrary.

Keywords

CTM procedure & practice; genuine use; discretion to accept additional evidence before the Board of Appeal; evidence submitted after expiry of the time limits.

Issue

Rehbein opposed a CTM application for a figurative mark, OUTBURST (see right) in class 25 based on an earlier German registration for the word mark OUTBURST in class 25. Rehbein was asked to furnish 'proof of use' of its earlier mark as it was more than five years old at the date of publication of the contested CTM.

The evidence submitted before the Opposition Division within the specified time-limit was deemed insufficient to demonstrate 'genuine use' of the earlier mark and the opposition was rejected. Rehbein appealed to the Board of Appeal and filed additional evidence. The Board of Appeal said it did not have discretion to accept the additional evidence because it was filed out of time and no new factor existed to justify the late submission. The Board of Appeal, therefore, upheld the Opposition Division's decision.

Ruling

The GC confirmed that the CTMR allows facts, arguments and evidence to be submitted after the expiry of a time limit where new factors exist, where there is no provision to the contrary and is it is justified and relevant to the outcome of the case. Evidence submitted for the first time in an appeal and after the expiry of the initial time limit provided for filing evidence is permissible provided it is intended to merely complement, strengthen and/or clarify the evidence that was originally submitted in the opposition proceedings. The GC concluded that the Board of Appeal did have discretion to take into account the evidence filed in the Appeal and that it was wrong not to consider it.

As the Board of Appeal's decision was made on an incomplete factual analysis of the evidence, the GC found that the contested decision must be annulled.

IP TRANSLATOR

Chartered Institute of Patent Attorneys v Registrar of Trade Marks
C-308/10, 19 June 2012

An application for a mark in the EU (national or Community) must identify, with sufficient clarity and precision, the goods and services to be protected so the competent authorities and competitors can determine the extent of the protection sought. It is essential to ensure that the desired goods/services are specifically claimed.

Keywords
CTM procedure & practice; specification of goods/services; Nice class headings; Communication 4/03.

Issue
On 16 June 2003 OHIM issued Communication 4/03 which stated that an application using the words of the Nice classification class heading included all the goods and services in that class. This conflicted with the approach taken by some EU states (including the UK) that if an application specifies certain goods/services, only they are included - the 'means what it says' approach.

In this test case, the UKIPO examined an application in accordance with Communication 4/03. It refused the application on the grounds that the mark IP TRANSLATOR was devoid of distinctive character as the class heading for class 41 ("Education; providing of training; entertainment; sporting and cultural activities") used in the application was deemed to include "all services" falling within the Nice Classification of class 41 which included "translation services". The Chartered Institute of Patent Attorneys (CIPA) appealed and certain questions were referred to the CJ.

Ruling
Applications in the EU have to specify the goods/services with sufficient clarity and precision to enable anyone, on that basis alone, to determine the exact extent of protection conferred by the mark. Whilst some of the Nice class headings may do so, many do not. If an applicant uses the class heading, it must specify whether protection is sought for the whole alphabetical list of the Nice classification or just the goods/services listed in the class heading. The CJ confused matters somewhat by referring to the "alphabetical list" of the Nice classification, which is not exhaustive, and could result in a narrower specification than "all the goods/services" actually included in a particular class. When filing a trade mark application the specific goods/services of interest should always be listed.

MEDINET

Franz Wilhelm Langguth Erben GmbH & Co KG v OHIM
T-378/11, 20 February 2013

The condition under Article 34(1) CTMR, that marks be identical to uphold a claim of seniority, must be interpreted restrictively. A claim of seniority from earlier national marks registered in colour by a later CTM, which did not stipulate any specific colour, was refused, as differences in colour did not constitute an insignificant difference.

Keywords

CTM procedure & practice; seniority; scope of protection; figurative marks; identity; Article 34(1) CTMR.

Issue

Franz Wilhelm applied for a CTM for the figurative sign MEDINET (right, above), and simultaneously claimed seniority from earlier national marks (right, below), pursuant to Article 34 CTMR. The examiner refused the claim of seniority, as did the Board of Appeal, who dismissed the appeal on the basis that the marks were not identical. The earlier marks were golden in colour whilst the CTM applied for did not state a specific colour.

The GC set out the three cumulative conditions for a seniority claim under Article 34 CTMR, namely that the applied for CTM must, relative to the earlier mark, be identical, cover or contain the same goods/services; and have the same proprietor. The latter two points were undisputed, so the GC's examination focused on assessing the identity of the marks in question.

Ruling

The criteria for assessing identity under Article 34(1) CTMR was held to be the same as that under Article 8(1)(a) CTMR (ie, where any differences between the marks are so insignificant that the average consumer may not notice them). The differences in colour did not constitute an insignificant difference, so the marks were not identical. Identity must be interpreted restrictively in case a lapse of an earlier mark enables a proprietor to continue having the same rights as if the earlier trade mark had remained registered. A claim for partial seniority was deemed inadmissible as it would render the condition of identity meaningless.

D YOUNG&CO
REGISTERED COMMUNITY DESIGNS

STABILO

Beifa Group Co Ltd v Schwan-Stabilo
Schwanhaüsser GmbH & Co KG & OHIM
T-148/08, 12 May 2010

Trade mark owners can enforce their marks against identical or similar designs but, where these trade marks are vulnerable to cancellation under the non-use provisions of the state in which the marks are protected, trade mark owners may have to prove use of their marks in order to successfully invalidate the design.

Keywords
Registered Community Designs; invalidity; comparisons with trade marks; proof of use; Article 25(1)(e) CDR.

Issue
Stabilo filed an application for invalidity against an RCD registered in respect of writing instruments on the basis of its prior German trade mark registration. The Cancellation Division and the Board of Appeal upheld Stabilo's application for invalidity and Beifa appealed to the GC.

Ruling
The GC held that it was possible for an RCD to contain different features to those depicted in the earlier trade mark, but to still constitute 'use' of the trade mark. Designs that are identical or similar to the trade marks in question can be challenged.

The RCD proprietor can request proof that the trade mark has been put to genuine use in the territory where it is protected where the mark is vulnerable to cancellation on the grounds of non-use. However, to do so, the request for proof of use must be made at the appropriate time before the first instance authority, and not introduced at the appeal stage.

The Cancellation Division had compared the design in question with a 3D trade mark, when in fact the trade mark relied on by Stabilo was a 2D figurative trade mark. The dispute had been decided on the basis of a trade mark that was not relied upon by Stabilo and therefore the Board of Appeal's decision to invalidate the design was annulled.

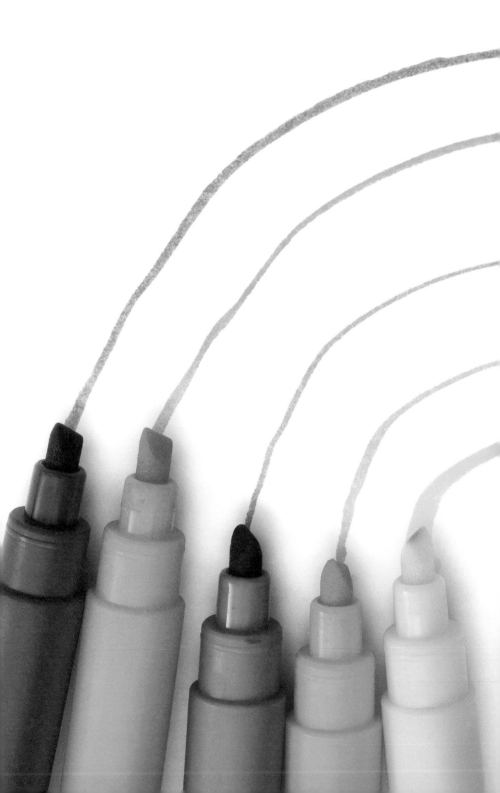

CONFERENCE SYSTEM UNITS

Shenzhen Taiden Industrial Co Ltd v Bosch
Security Systems BV & OHIM
T-153/08, 22 June 2010

Anyone who used the goods in question was held to be
a so-called 'informed user'.

Keywords

Registered Community Designs; invalidity; individual character; Article 4(1) CDR;
Article 6(1)(b) CDR; Article 6(2) CDR; Article 7(1) CDR; Article 25(1)(b) CDR.

Issue

Shenzhen Taiden applied for an RCD in relation to communications equipment.
Bosch applied to invalidate the design on the grounds that the design was not
new and lacked individual character, as required under Article 4 CDR. Bosch
relied on its own registered design in relation to units for conference systems.
OHIM rejected the invalidity action but the Board of Appeal held that Shenzhen's
design lacked individual character and invalidated the design.

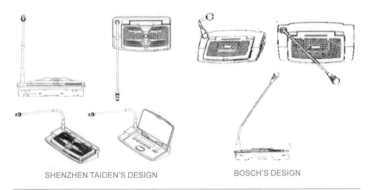

SHENZHEN TAIDEN'S DESIGN   BOSCH'S DESIGN

Ruling

The GC held that the informed user was any person who used conference
units with microphones.

The GC found that the sole difference between the two designs in question
was the lid of the hinged speaker, but the importance of this was reduced
because when the device was in use, the visibility of the conference unit's
cover was limited.

The GC found that both designs created the same overall impression and,
as such, Shenzhen Taiden's design was invalid.

INTERNAL COMBUSTION ENGINE

Kwang Yang Motor Co Ltd v OHIM
T-10/08 & T-11/08, 09 September 2011

In relation to a component part of a complex product, the test for individual character over a prior art design involves, first of all, deciding what is the normal use of the component part and which features of the component part remain visible during that normal use. Only then can individual character be assessed against those features which remain visible.

Keywords

Registered Community Designs; component part of complex product; features visible in normal use; individual character; Article 4 CDR; Article 6 CDR; Article 25(1)(b) CDR.

Issue

Honda filed invalidity actions against two related RCDs belonging to Kwang Yang. The issues involved were essentially the same for the two cases. Honda lost at first instance but won before the Board of Appeal. It argued that each RCD lacked individual character relative to a prior US design patent. The design of each RCD was for an internal combustion engine, which was a 'component part of a complex product' because the engine would, in use, be incorporated in a bigger piece of apparatus such as a lawnmower. The Board of Appeal decided that the features of the engine which would remain visible in 'normal use' lacked individual character relative to the prior art and that the differences in detail of the features were not significant because the engine designer had a high degree of design freedom.

Ruling

The GC upheld the Board of Appeal's decision in both cases and confirmed its analysis. The GC placed emphasis on the fact that, in normal use of the engine, it is primarily the features of the upper side of the engine that remain visible when the engine is incorporated in a lawnmower because a user (standing behind the lawnmower) would look down onto the upper side of the engine. The features of the upper side did not produce a different overall impression on the informed user. The GC dismissed the argument of Kwang Yang that the informed user was a manufacturer of lawnmowers. The GC held that the informed user was anyone who used lawnmowers.

WATCHES

Sphere Time v OHIM
T-68/10, 14 June 2011

The GC approved the practice, set out in OHIM's examination guidelines for RCD applications, of using dashed or dotted lines to illustrate features of the design for which protection is not being sought but which provide context for the features shown in solid line.

Keywords

Registered Community Designs; novelty; individual character; prior art designs; Article 4 CDR; Article 6 CDR; Article 7 CDR; Article 61-63 CDR.

Issue

Punch SAS had filed an invalidity action against Sphere Time's RCD relating to a design for a watch attached to a lanyard, alleging lack of novelty or individual character relative to a prior art design. Punch won at first instance at OHIM, and the decision of the Invalidity Division was maintained by the Board of Appeal. Sphere Time appealed to the GC. Apart from contesting novelty and individual character, Sphere Time also alleged that the Board of Appeal had 'misused' its powers by not correctly evaluating the arguments and evidence that had been put forward by Sphere Time.

Ruling

The GC dismissed the appeal, and said that there had been no 'misuse' of powers because the Board of Appeal had not restricted the right of Sphere Time to mount a defence and had stated adequate reasons. When evaluating the scope of the RCD, the GC noted that the design was depicted using the technique of showing some (claimed) features in solid line and some (disclaimed) features in dashed line. The GC noted that this practice is mentioned in the examination guidelines for pending applications as being one of the acceptable techniques for illustrating the context in which the design (the claimed solid-line features) may be used, and the GC approved this practice for depicting a design. The GC then maintained that the Board of Appeal had correctly evaluated that the informed user would consider that the design of the RCD had only negligible differences relative to the cited prior art design and thus, the RCD had been correctly held to lack individual character.

RAPPER

PepsiCo Inc v Grupo Promer Mon Graphic SA (OHIM)
C-281/10, 20 October 2011

The 'informed user' in registered design law is a
particularly observant individual who occupies an
intermediate position on the spectrum between an
average, uninterested individual and an individual who is
an expert interested in even minor design differences. The
case also provides helpful guidance on the relevant test for
assessing what constitutes a 'different overall impression'.

Keywords
Registered Community Designs; prior RCD; different overall impression;
informed user; Article 5 CDR; Article 6 CDR; Article 10 CDR; Article 25(1)(d) CDR.

Issue
PepsiCo filed an RCD application for a promotional item described as a
'rapper'. The RCD was contested by Grupo on the basis of an earlier right.
OHIM declared the design invalid but the Board of Appeal overturned the
decision. On further appeal, the GC overturned the Board of Appeal's decision.

Ruling
The CJ upheld the GC's decision. In relation to assessing
individual character of an RCD, relative to an earlier design,
the CJ concurred that the test for 'individual character'
(ie, whether the design in suit produces
a different overall impression on the
informed user relative to the prior
design) involves considering that the
informed user is a person who occupies
an intermediate position on the
spectrum between the 'average
consumer' of trade mark law and an
expert in the designs in question.

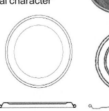

GRUPO DESIGN   PEPSICO DESIGN

The informed user is a user who is particularly observant because of their
personal experience or their extensive knowledge of the sector in question and,
when comparing the designs, they show a relatively high degree of attention to
differences between them. The CJ held that the comparison of the designs
would often be a side-by-side comparison of the two designs.

TRAFFIC BOLLARDS

Celaya Emparanza y Galdos Internacional SA (Cegasa)
v Proyectos Integrales de Balizamientos SL (Proin)
C-488/10, 16 February 2012

A later RCD does not provide a shield against being held
to infringe an earlier RCD belonging to another party.

Keywords

Registered Community Designs; effect of existence of a later RCD on
infringement of an earlier RCD; Article 19(1) CDR.

Issue

Cegasa owned an RCD consisting of a "beacon-like marker used for traffic
signalling purposes" and had accused Proin of infringement. Proin then
applied for and obtained its own RCD relating to the product which had been
accused of infringement. Proin then argued that, because Article 19(1) CDR
confers on the owner of an RCD "the exclusive right to use (the RCD)", the
Proin product (being protected by the later RCD) could not infringe the earlier
Cegasa RCD. To hold that there was infringement, would, according to Proin,
deprive it of its own "exclusive right to use" its (later) RCD. Proin also
considered that it is irrelevant that its "exclusive right to use" is in conflict with
Cegasa's "exclusive right to stop" infringement of the earlier (Cegasa) RCD.
Interestingly, Cegasa did not attempt to invalidate the later (Proin) RCD,
which, if successful, would have removed Proin's defensive line of argument.
The Spanish court hearing the case applied to the CJ for a preliminary ruling
on the line of argument based on Article 19(1) CDR.

Ruling

The CJ essentially decided that the earlier RCD trumps the later RCD on "the
priority principle, under which the
earlier RCD takes precedence over
later RCDs". In other words, Proin's
defence was not valid and the right
of the proprietor of an earlier RCD
to "the exclusive right ... to
prevent any third party" applies
even when that third party is
the proprietor of a later RCD.

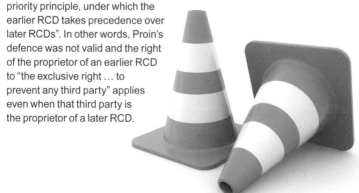

SITTING GOBLIN

Herbert Neuman, Andoni Galdeano del Sel & OHIM
v José Manuel Baena Grupo, SA
Joined cases C-101/11 & C-102/11, 18 October 2012

The informed user of Community Design law is
particularly observant, with personal experience or
extensive knowledge of the relevant sector.

Keywords

Registered Community Design; informed user; Article 6 CDR; Article 25(1) CDR.

Issue

Baena Grupo owned the design (below left), against which Herbert Neuman
and Andoni Galdeano del Sel submitted a declaration of invalidity based on a
lack of individual character (Article 6 CDR) when compared with their earlier
trade mark (below right), because the design included a distinctive sign as
owned by them (Article 25(1)(e) CDR).

The Cancellation Division upheld the declaration of invalidity on the basis of the
Article 25(1)(e) CDR claim. When appealed, the Board of Appeal held that this
was not correct, although the design was still invalid on grounds of lacking
individual character as it did not create a different impression on the informed
user (ie, the Article 25(1)(e) CDR claim was rejected, but the claim based on a
lack of individual character under Article 6 CDR was successful). This was
appealed again, and the GC annulled the decision. Both the applicants for
invalidity and OHIM appealed to the CJ.

Ruling

The CJ dismissed both appeals and in doing so reiterated its views in PepsiCo v
Grupo Promer Mon Graphic SA (OHIM) (RAPPER, page 190), stating that whilst
there is no formal definition of the informed user it should be taken that they are
particularly observant, with personal experience or extensive knowledge of the
relevant sector. It was also noted that where possible, the informed user would
make a direct comparison of the relevant designs, but that such a comparison
may not always be practical or common – in such circumstances the GC had
been entitled to base its reasoning on the informed user's imperfect recollection
of the overall impression produced by the two images above.

D YOUNG&CO
INDEX

Chapter contents

Index by section

Absolute grounds / Graphical representation

Absolute grounds / Descriptive & non-distinctive marks

Absolute grounds / Acquired distinctiveness

Absolute grounds / Slogans

Index by section cont.

Infringement & opposition grounds / Reputation

Infringement & opposition grounds / Keywords

Infringement & opposition grounds / Comparative advertising

Index by section cont.

Index by section cont.

Registered Community Designs

Index by case

Index by case cont.

Index by case

Index by case cont.

Index by case cont.